Why Work?

How the Federal Entitlements and Tax Systems Equalize Income and Wealth

By Allen Buckley and Jonathan Godbey

WHY WORK? HOW THE FEDERAL ENTITLEMENTS AND TAX SYSTEMS EQUALIZE INCOME AND WEALTH

Written by Allen Buckley and Jonathan Godbey

Table of Contents

Dedication

The authors dedicate this book to their daughters in hope of making their futures, and the futures of all young people, brighter.

Forward

This book will attempt to explain how the federal entitlements and tax systems create disincentives to work, advance, save, and be responsible for a large percentage of the American population. Simply put, for a large segment of the population, working and saving doesn't pay.

Historically, Americans have valued hard work and self-reliance. However, the current federal system of entitlements and taxes has made these objectives unattractive for a large segment of the population by decreasing one's standard of living for exhibiting these qualities. The existing system is destroying the fabric of what has made America great while making our people weaker and causing our system to become semi-socialized.

We, the authors, consider ourselves to be fiscally conservative individuals. However, we do not believe we could reasonably be deemed to be "right wingers." We do not oppose a government safety net of some reasonable nature. Also, we do not oppose a reasonably progressive income tax system. However, we believe the existing system of entitlements, when coupled with the tax system, produces unfair results and destroys incentive to work, advance, save, and be responsible for a large segment of the population. This book will present facts and figures to explain why we believe our thoughts are correct, such that no reasonable person would disagree.

The book introduces four typical Americans at various positions of the socio-economic scale and demonstrates how the federal entitlements and tax system affects their lives. The 2013 federal and Georgia income tax systems were used, as it is unclear what the 2014 landscape will hold at the time of publication. Entitlements are those in existence in late 2013 and early 2014, including entitlements supplied by Obamacare. The book assumes that these provisions will remain in effect indefinitely and have been in effect for the pertinent past. The applicable state law is Georgia law unless specified otherwise.

Chapter 1

Core Principles

The nation is now sharply divided along partisan lines. Discussions of serious issues are marred by distrust and political gamesmanship. The authors are not interested in adding to the noise. Rather, we seek to start an evidence- and logic-based discussion that we hope will result in a stronger nation. We begin with four principles, which we believe most Americans support. We seek to convince the reader who believes in these principles that there are major flaws in the current tax and entitlements systems. No one person or group designed the system. We believe the outcomes of the system are contrary to what any person of goodwill would want, whether they are conservative, liberal, or anywhere in between. No one could look at it and say, "It is good." The core principles of the authors' beliefs follow.

There should be a safety net. Reasonable people of goodwill can disagree on exactly how much financial assistance should be made available to people in need. Until approximately 80 years ago, this need was filled almost exclusively by charities. The authors take no position in that discussion, including the degree to which it should be filled by charity versus the government, other than to affirm the need for some type of safety net. However, for the non-elderly who are able to work, it should only be provided to those who work or, in good faith, try to work.

The safety net should be secure for future generations. It's easy to recognize the needs of people we can see. It's not as easy to consider the needs of people yet to be born. Every dollar spent today is one less dollar that may be spent tomorrow. We must not kill the goose that laid the golden egg. Today's safety net must not destroy tomorrow's government.

Work and saving should *always* be rewarded. The United States should be a country in which anyone who is willing to work hard and save money can climb the economic ladder. While the dream of absolute economic fairness is unattainable and undefinable, the system should be designed to help people climb, not hinder their ascent. Someone who acts irresponsibly should not be rewarded at the expense of the responsible.

The rules of the game should be easily understood. A baseball player and his manager know the rules of the game. They can develop a strategy to win based on those rules. The same is true for football, basketball, soccer, chess, checkers, and every other sport or game played by children or professionals. No one or virtually no one understands the entitlement system as currently in place. No one struggling to feed, clothe, and shelter a family has the time and resources to learn the system and respond to the rules in a rational manner.

The following graph applies to married couples with two children making $50,000 per year or more. They will keep 55 to 65 percent of their incremental earnings over $50,000. Assuming an average net take-home pay percent of 60, an economist would say that their marginal tax rate is 40 percent, which means they pay 40 cents in taxes for every additional $1 of earnings. One could argue that they should be able to keep more or less. That is a discussion for another book. If we assume the increase in take home pay is fair for this family, what is fair for the family attempting to climb out of poverty to the median income level? It is important to note in the following graph that take home pay always increases as gross income increases. And it increases at an almost constant rate.

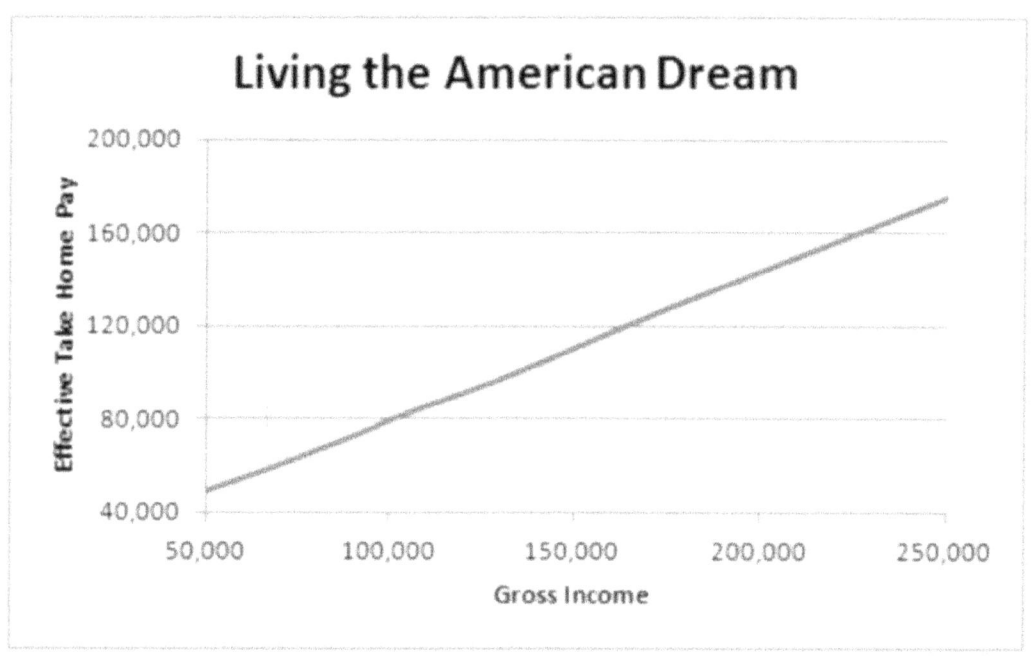

The steeper the line in the above picture, the more money the family

gets to keep. Except perhaps for a reasonable floor, shouldn't the line for

those below the median household income be the same or at least never be

downward sloping? (Note: The graphs provided in this chapter assume

that all significant entitlements available under the federal umbrella are

applied.)

The next graph shows the increased, effective take home pay for a

similar family of four who is trying to climb out of poverty. (Effective take-

home pay means the amount the family would have for a given level of

earnings if all entitlements were paid in cash.) An annual family income of

$10,000 would be complemented with entitlements and tax credits (exclusive of Medicaid) bringing the family's effective take home pay to $33,446. If the mom or dad or both work hard and increase their total earnings to $25,000, the family benefits. Their $15,000 pay increase results in their effective take home pay increasing by $15,572 to $49,018. Their marginal tax rate is negative 3.8 percent. Work pays. The family is able to climb well above the federal poverty level of $23,550.

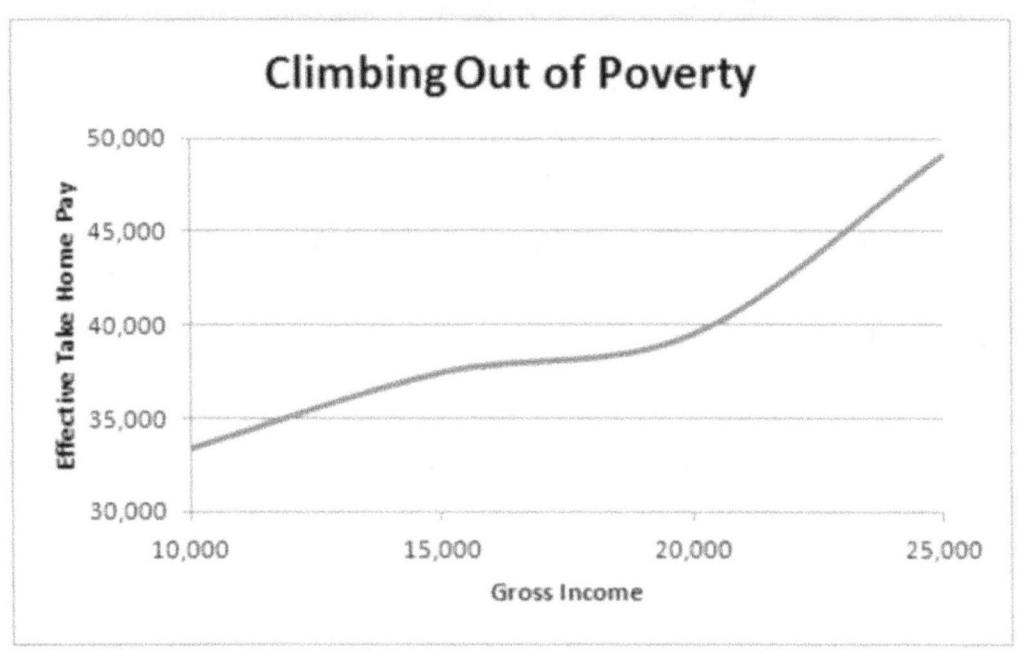

The following graph shows this same family stuck in "the ditch." It is an area where standard of living actually diminishes for people climbing out of poverty toward the median income. As they work harder and increase their pay, entitlements are decreased and their effective take home pay *decreases*. *The family is worse off.* It would take over 23 years of consecutive 3 percent raises to reach a gross income of $50,000, which is almost the median household income. Then, the family would only be $328 better off. Their marginal tax rate is **98.7 percent**. If the family could realize this 100 percent pay raise in a year or two, then it would not be significantly harmed. However, most families must climb the economic ladder slowly. As this family's gross income increases from $30,000 to $35,000, its marginal tax rate is an unbelievable **143.1 percent**. Thus, a $5,000 pay raise would reduce their take-home pay by $2,156.50. The family would be significantly worse off by accepting the raise. They are stuck in the ditch. The system helps people climb out of poverty, but then traps them there.

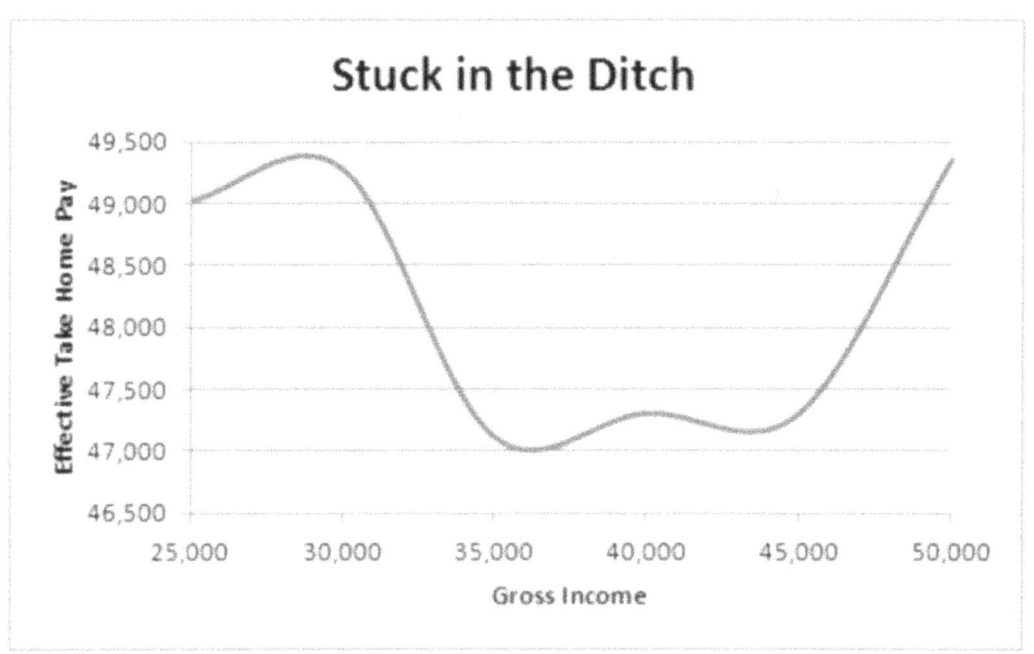

As explained below, while the federal entitlements and tax systems cause work not to pay for many middle class individuals and families, other entitlements, particularly federal financial aid for college and nursing home care, can wipe out the assets of persons who have saved while those who did not save receive substantially greater government benefits. A saver can potentially lose tens of thousands of dollars to pay college costs while a non-saver with the same income but no savings can pay a small fraction of what the saver paid.

Chapter 2

The Entitlements Problem

As a percentage of the size of the economy of the United States (i.e., the U.S. Gross Domestic Product, or GDP), actual traditional "government" spending has not changed much in many years. Here, traditional government spending includes expenditures for the armed forces, national roads and highways, the federal legal system, the EPA, and other federal agencies, such as the IRS, and the like. However, overall federal spending has increased substantially as a percent of GDP in recent years, and it is expected to increase dramatically in future years. But, the anticipated growth is not attributable to traditional government functions. Rather, it is due to increased entitlement spending.

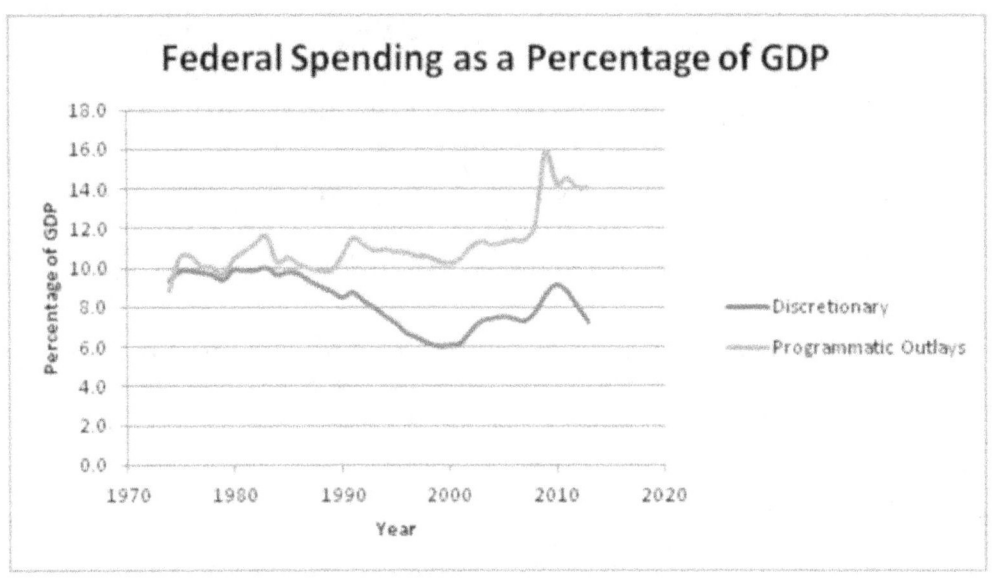

Source: Congressional Budget Office (CBO)

The CBO, the nonpartisan federal arm in charge of independent budgetary and economic issues support for Congress, describes discretionary and mandatory spending as follows:

> Discretionary spending is the part of federal spending that lawmakers control through annual appropriation acts. Mandatory spending, in contrast, occurs each year without such legislation; spending for mandatory programs is generally determined by setting the programs parameters, such as eligibility rules and benefit formulas, rather than by appropriating specific amounts each year.

Discretionary spending includes costs relating to defense programs, military personnel, and procurement. Nondefense discretionary spending includes education, training, employment and social services, transportation, income security (mostly housing) and health-related research and public health. It also includes law enforcement and judicial services, veterans' benefits and services (mainly health care) and international affairs.

Entitlements comprise the vast majority of mandatory spending. Entitlements are cash and noncash benefits granted to citizens and residents by law. Most entitlements are provided by the federal government. For 2013, mandatory spending cost the federal government $2.032 trillion. Discretionary spending totaled $1.201 trillion.

Some entitlements, such as Medicaid benefits, are jointly provided by the federal government and state governments. The federal government is the primary funding source for Medicaid in all of the states. According to www.Medicaid.gov, the Federal Medicaid Assistance Percentage varies from 50 percent for wealthier states to 75 percent for states with lower per capita incomes. As a condition of providing Medicaid funding, the federal government requires that states do certain things with respect to money they receive from the federal government (i.e., strings are attached). According to the CBO, $265 billion of Medicaid grants were issued to the states in 2013.

For many years, the debt of the U.S. government has been growing as a percent of GDP. It has been growing because federal revenues from taxes and other sources have failed to keep pace with spending growth. In 1980, total federal debt was approximately 33 percent of GDP. Today, it is greater than 103 percent of GDP.

Since World War II, annual federal revenues have ranged between 14 and 21 percent of GDP. While tax laws have caused some of the variances over the years, the primary driver of increased or decreased revenue has been the strength of the economy. In prosperous years (e.g., 2000), revenues are relatively high. In recession years (e.g., 2009), revenues are relatively low. (In 2000, federal revenues equaled 20.6 percent of GDP; in 2009, the percent was 15.1.)

The growth of entitlements is largely due to demographics. After World War II, many people married and had children. Large families were common. The first baby boomers, born in 1946, became eligible for America's two most costly entitlement programs, Social Security and

Medicare, upon attaining age 65 in 2011. The 2013 costs of Social Security and Medicare were, respectively, $808 billion and $585 billion. For 2013, total federal revenue was $2.77 trillion. Since 2011, the group of persons eligible for Medicare and Social Security has been growing rapidly. As the baby boom officially ended in 1964, there will be approximately 15 more years of retiring boomers being added to the ranks.

Financial magazines and reporters have taken note of the problem. On November 13, 2013, www.forbes.com reported in "Washington's Indisputable Crisis: Entitlement Programs Cost 92 Percent of Federal Revenues," that "[t]he federal government is spending 92 cents out of every dollar it receives on entitlement programs, plus interest on the federal debt." It should be noted that the final entitlements figures for 2013 were slightly less than those originally budgeted.

The following chart lists anticipated federal revenues, spending, and debt (exclusive of debt owed to Social Security and similar intergovernmental debt under existing laws). Most of the anticipated future debt is due to entitlements and the inability of revenue to keep pace with spending increases.

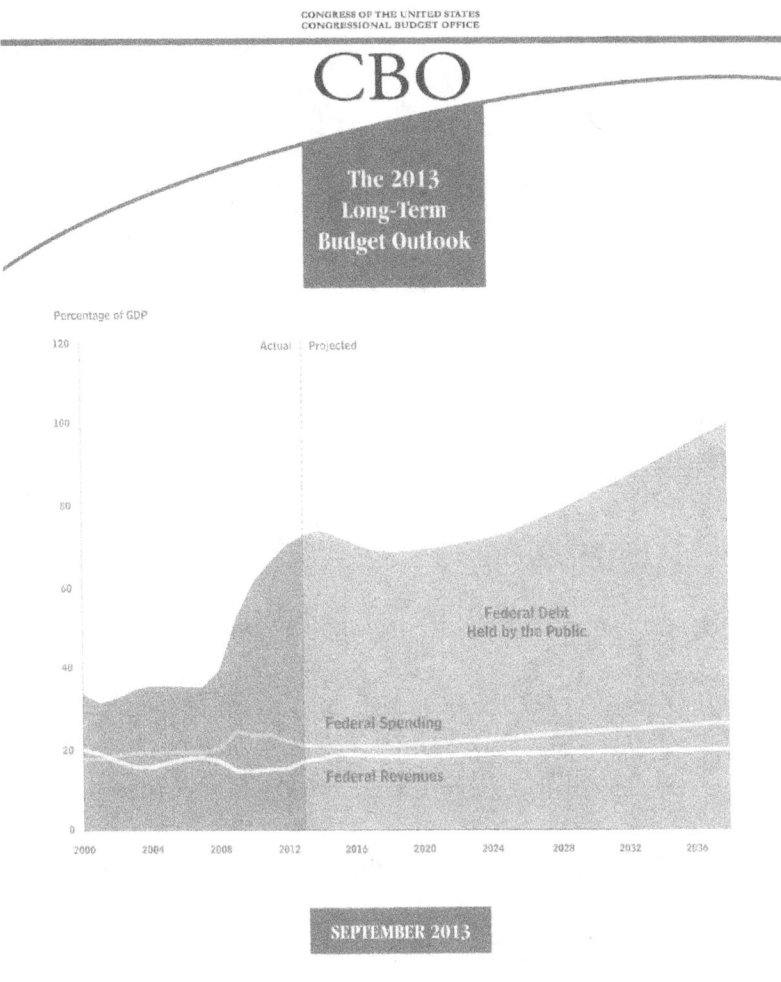

CONGRESS OF THE UNITED STATES
CONGRESSIONAL BUDGET OFFICE

CBO

The 2013
Long-Term
Budget Outlook

SEPTEMBER 2013

As a percentage of average personal disposable income, federal debt has grown from 46 percent in 1980 to 138 percent in 2012.

If spending increases and taxes don't increase to match the spending increases, the result is additional debt. Normally, as a debtor becomes a bigger risk, he or she must pay a higher rate of interest to creditors to account for the increased risk. To date, the United States has not experienced interest rate pressure from creditors. In fact, because the United States has the largest economy in the world and is still deemed a relatively safe place to invest, the Federal Reserve Bank has been able to push interest rates to all-time lows. Doing so helps produce economic activity, and it also helps reduce the interest expense of the federal government.

The Federal Reserve Bank has the power to print money (or, as it is often described, "buy bonds"). This power has been used extensively recently, and for many recent years $85 billion of bonds were purchased each month (i.e., $1.02 trillion per year). Total GDP is now approximately $17 trillion. The new money has helped the stock markets, thus also improving consumer confidence. However, the risk of significant inflation in the near future exists. Given that the Federal Reserve Bank can print money to buy U.S. government securities, it would seem that things could stay comfortable for quite a while. However, our own government financial authorities tell us otherwise.

The CBO has said for many years that our nation's finances are "unsustainable." Given the preceding chart, that description is somewhat lame. The federal government's audit arm, the Government Accountability Office (GAO) was more alarming in its 2007 (pre-Great Recession and its related debt explosion) statement: "GAO's long-term simulations continue to show ever larger deficits resulting in a federal debt burden that ultimately spirals out of control."

In the future, either entitlements will be substantially reduced or some combination of entitlements reduction and tax increases will occur. Otherwise, our nation's debts will spiral out of control. If the debts spiral out of control, the financial system will collapse. If the financial system collapses, it is hard to imagine how any portion of the system will remain. Presumably, a market economy would come into existence immediately, with people performing trade without a currency to simplify trade. The weak (including many of the elderly) would be at the mercy of the strong.

Most of the anticipated growth in debt relates to Medicaid, Medicare, and Social Security. Thus, those are the primary entitlements that must be targeted to solve the massive problem. However, for reasons explained below, the remainder of the entitlements system needs to be reformed as well in order to eliminate disincentives to work, advance, save, and be responsible.

What is happening in the United States is normal for a democracy. A famous quote that some have (perhaps incorrectly) attributed to 18th century Scottish scholar Alexander Frasier Tytler is: "A democracy cannot exist as a permanent form of government. It can only exist until the voters discover they can vote themselves largesse from the public treasury. From then on, the majority votes for the candidates promising the most from the public treasury, with the result that a democracy always collapses over loose fiscal policy, followed by a dictatorship. . . ." Whether Mr. Tytler said this or someone else deserves the credit, it appears to be a wise statement, as many democracies throughout the world are headed for financial catastrophe.

Chapter 3

The Home

Eleanor felt uneasy as her son, David, drove her into the entrance of the Don't Worry, Be Happy Nursing Home. "Tell me again exactly why I have to come here?" she asked David.

"Because the assisted living experts said it was time for you to go; we had no choice," was his response. "We've been through all this several times; let's make the best of it."

David grabbed Eleanor's walker from the back seat and helped her from the passenger side of his car. She slowly made her way to the front desk of her new home.

After completing some paperwork, Eleanor and David were escorted to Eleanor's room by an attendant. The worker then told Eleanor to make herself comfortable and said that someone would come by later to explain the lay of the land. Although two beds existed, it was apparent that no one else was staying in the room. Eleanor changed her clothes in the bathroom and returned to talk to David. "Well, what do you think?" asked David.

"Ah, it's OK," was his mother's reply. "At least I have a window."

She and David looked out the window at the thick group of trees and small pond just outside Eleanor's room.

Some birds were sitting on the edge of the pond. David said: "Perhaps you'll see some deer." "Yes, perhaps," replied Eleanor.

"I'm sure you'll make some friends, here, Mom," said David. "There's got to be a number of patients here who, like you, are in really good shape — I mean, really don't need to be here."

"Yes, I'm sure there are a few residents who still have their minds. Perhaps I'll be able to relate to them . . . but perhaps not. Time will tell."

After about an hour, Eleanor said: "There's no reason for you to continue to hang around, son; I'll be alright."

"I know you'll be fine, Mom. Can I help you unpack . . . or walk you around?" replied David.

"No, thank you. I can handle unpacking myself; I'll do my own exploring," said Eleanor.

David continued: "You know I live less than 30 minutes away, so I'll be coming to visit you regularly."

"I know, I know you will," responded Eleanor.

David hugged Eleanor and departed.

Eleanor sat and stared out the window for several minutes. She could not help but think: *So this is where I must spend my final days?* She wished to be outside, on the edge of the pond with the birds — in nature.

Eleanor unpacked. In the process, she noted a loose leaf notebook on the desk titled List of Patients. She perused it. One name caught her attention: Diane Brown. She recalled her high school friend, Diane Given, who had later married and taken the last name of her husband, Brown. Eleanor had not seen Diane in decades and wondered: *Could it be her?*

Eleanor noted the room number for Diane Brown. Perhaps later, Eleanor would take a walk and see if it was her old friend.

Eleanor's thoughts were interrupted when a nurse walked into the room. The nurse explained how things worked at the home. She described the rules, meal times, and the like. Eleanor inquired about walking throughout the facility. The nurse informed her that she could do so if she felt up to it.

After the discussion, it was time for dinner (5:00 p.m.). Eleanor made her way to the cafeteria. She sat and was waited on by an aide. She looked over the room as patients slowly filtered in. She thought to herself: *I think I'm in better shape than most of them.* Being new, no one joined Eleanor at her table. After she ate, she walked to the room assigned to Diane Brown. She glanced in the room. No one was there. Perhaps she was at dinner, and Eleanor had just missed her. Eleanor would return later.

Eleanor walked throughout the facility for almost an hour. Then, she returned to the Diane Brown's room. Therein, she saw a woman whom she recognized as her old friend. Diane was lying in her bed, watching television.

Eleanor knocked. "Have time for an old friend?" she inquired.

Diane looked up. "Oh my goodness, is that Ela Davis?" responded Diane.

"You mean, Ela Roberts, for the past 48 years." Eleanor walked to Diane, bent over and hugged her. The two began to chat.

After about a half hour of catching up, Diane said: "There are two other girls from Westlake High School staying here, Barbie Holmes and Tracy O'Reilly."

Eleanor asked, "Are those their high school names or their married names?"

"High school. Barbie's last name is now Morgan; Tracy's name hasn't changed." Diane continued, "We meet for lunch almost every day. You need to join us."

"Sounds good, although I honestly don't remember either one of them."

Diane explained: "Barbie was a majorette; I'm not sure what Tracy was into at the time—I didn't recall her either; Barbie knew her fairly well and she introduced us."

The two talked a little more. Finally, Eleanor said, "I think it's time for me to head back to my crib. What time is lunch tomorrow?"

"We usually meet pretty late—around noon."

"Great, I'll see you then."

———

The next day, Eleanor arrived at the cafeteria for the planned lunch just before noon. She was curious whether she would remember Barbie and Tracy. Diane entered the cafeteria with another woman. She saw Eleanor and approached her.

"Ela Roberts, formerly Ela Davis, I wish to introduce you to Barbie Morgan, formerly Barbie Holmes, Westlake High Class of 1955," said Diane.

"I remember you," said Eleanor.

"And I recall you as well," responded Barbie. They spoke briefly, and then Diane directed them to a table where a woman was already seated.

"Ela Roberts, meet Tracy O'Reilly, Westlake High School Class of 1955," Diane said.

"My goodness," said Eleanor. "I'm sorry, but I don't recall our ever having been acquainted."

Tracy responded: "I knew you, but we probably said two words to each other the entire time we were in high school."

"Well, let's get to know each other now," said Eleanor.

The women sat and ordered. Over lunch, they told their stories.

Eleanor explained that she had married her college sweetheart, Frank, five years after they both had graduated from the University of Georgia. She said that Frank, who died two years ago, had started his own plumbing business just out of college. She explained how Frank's parents were upset that he did not use his college degree in a more professional manner. Eleanor said that Frank was never into appearances and that he created a very successful plumbing business called "Frank Fixes It." The other women said they were familiar with the local business. Diane noted that she had used its services many times. Eleanor concluded by talking about her two children, one who had graduated from Cornell University and the other who had graduated from Auburn University. She noted that one child was five years older than the other child.

Eleanor's financial situation (most of which was not told to the other women): During their most productive years, Frank and Eleanor averaged $250,000 of income from Frank Fixes It. Eleanor has a home with a value of $750,000. She has no debts. She also has $200,000 in stocks and bonds and $800,000 of assets in an IRA that she inherited from Frank.

It was Diane's turn. Diane explained that she had attended Kent State University, where she had received her nursing degree. She said she attended Kent because her father was an alum, and she really wanted to live somewhere different than Georgia. However, upon graduating, she returned to the sunny South, where she later married her husband (now deceased). Diane explained that her husband was a teacher. He had slowly worked his way up through the ranks of the Cobb County School System. Diane told the women how she had worked part time while raising her two children and that she had returned to work basically full time when they were both in school. Finally, she said that one of her children had graduated from Purdue University and the other one had graduated from Georgia Tech. She noted that her children were born four years apart.

Diane said that she had lived in the huge Wee-Land Homes subdivision of Cobb County for many decades. She said that she and her husband had first leased a home there for many years. Later, they had bought the home from their landlord. Diane then said: "It came as a shock to me to learn that Barbie and Tracy lived in the same subdivision for most of the years that I had lived there. The place is so big; I don't think I ever ran across them."

Diane mentioned one of her best friends from elementary school who attended a nearby high school. She noted how her friend was also a nurse and that her friend had also worked part time while raising her children. Diane said that, coincidentally, her friend's spouse was also a Cobb County School System teacher. Diane noted how she and her husband had always worked, saved, and vacationed and lived modestly, while her friend and her husband dined out regularly and took many luxurious vacations. Otherwise, they had the same standard of living as Diane and her husband. She noted how it was somewhat aggravating to her and her husband that they had worked and saved but had never got ahead of her carefree friend and her husband. Diane said: "I recall her and her husband taking two-week cruises to the Caribbean and the

Mediterranean; my husband and I were lucky if we went to the beach for one week each year." Diane noted that her friend and her husband also had two children, but her children were born one year apart.

Diane's Financial Situation (most of which was not told to other women): When only her husband worked, they averaged $45,000–$60,000 of income per year. Years later, when they both worked, their average was $100,000–$115,000. Her assets include a home with a value of $350,000 that is subject to a $50,000 home equity line of credit (HELOC). She receives pension benefits of $2,500/month. Her other assets are $40,000 in cash and CDs and $175,000 of equity in a rental home that she and her husband had purchased and rented for many years. The HELOC debt was incurred in part to help finance the college education of her children. (The original debt amount was higher.) Diane's friend, who had attended a nearby high school, has the same next worth except she has no cash or CDs and no rental home.

It was Barbie's turn. She explained that she had started college but had eventually dropped out and taken various jobs. Later, she married and had two children. While her children were in school, she had worked part time at a local department store. Her (now deceased) husband had not attended college. He had worked as a clerk for Home Depot for many years. Later, he had moved up the ladder to become an assistant manager. Both of her children graduated from the University of Georgia. The children were born six years apart.

Barbie's Financial Situation (most of which was not told to the other women): The average gross income of her and her husband had been in the $40,000 to $60,000 range for many years. Prior to entering the nursing home, she rented a house (recently for $1,100 per month), just as she and her husband had done for decades. Her net worth is comprised of cash and CDs worth $10,000 and IRA assets of $80,000 that she inherited from her husband upon his death.

Finally, Tracy told her story. "I was, essentially, a burnout in school," she admitted. "I didn't follow the rules, and I certainly didn't want to go to college, so I didn't go. That's probably a big part of the reason that few people remember me. I was a nonconformist. However, over the years, I came to value the education I never had. I impressed upon my kids that education is important." She took a job out of high school as a waitress at the local IHOP. Later, she moved to Waffle House. Over the years, she had worked various jobs. In her 20s, she married, but it did not last. She, too, has two children. One child was born during her marriage. The other one was born out of wedlock. Both of her children attended and graduated from reputable universities. Tracy bragged: "While I never went to college, both of my kids graduated from really great schools—Duke and UGA—and I didn't pay a dime."

Tracy's Financial Situation (most of which was not told to the other women): Tracy's annual earnings averaged $15,000-20,000, and never exceeded $25,000. Also, she received $400 of child support monthly for many years, until her oldest child turned age 18. She has no assets a net worth of zero.

Chapter 4

Entitlements, Taxes, and Standard of Living

It should be noted that, with the exception of Eleanor, the lifestyles of the women depicted in the preceding chapter are relatively similar. Specifically, Diane, Barbie, and Tracy had all lived in the same neighborhood, and their children had all attended and graduated from reputable universities. Yet, their education, income, and net worth levels were significantly different. How can that be? It can be because the federal entitlements system, when coupled with the federal tax system, provides for it.

And what about Diane's friend who lived a much easier life than Diane and her husband yet seemed to be on the same financial footing as Diane and her husband? How did that come about? It came about because the federal entitlements system provides for it.

The following table shows the estimated net income of a family of four under the federal entitlements and tax system, coupled with the Georgia's income tax system under expanded Medicaid as provided for by

Patient Protection and Affordable Care Act, as amended by the Health

Care and Education Reconciliation Act of 2010 (hereafter, "Obamacare" or

the "ACA"). As explained in Chapter 7, Obamacare greatly expanded

Medicaid eligibility, but a 2012 U.S. Supreme Court decision allowed states

to forgo expansion without losing federal funding. Obamacare's

"individual mandate" requires certain persons to obtain health insurance

coverage. The net income figures in the bottom row of the table show the

estimated income available to the family after taxes and the net cost of

subsidized items are subtracted from their gross income. (Note: All figures

that are shown in this chapter assume all income is properly reported to

government authorities. To the extent income is not reported, lifestyle is

greater than what is provided.)

Net Income for a Family of Four with ACA Medicaid Expansion

Gross pay	10,000	20,000	30,000	40,000	50,000	60,000	70,000	80,000	90,000	100,000
FICA	765	1,530	2,295	3,060	3,825	4,590	5,355	6,120	6,885	7,650
Federal income tax	0	0	221	1,223	2,441	3,941	5,441	6,941	8,441	9,941
EIC & child credit	-5,060	-7,372	-5,865	-3,759	-2,000	-2,000	-2,000	-2,000	-2,000	-2,000
State tax	0	69	559	1,159	1,759	2,359	2,959	3,559	4,159	4,759
Net after tax	14,295	25,773	32,790	38,317	43,975	51,110	58,245	65,380	72,515	79,650
Health Care	0	0	0	11,178	11,178	11,178	11,178	11,178	11,178	11,178
ACA Credit	0	0	0	9,213	7,813	6,265	4,584	3,578	2,628	0
Net after ACA	14,295	25,773	32,790	36,352	40,610	46,197	51,651	57,780	63,965	68,472
Housing Rent	2,568	5,568	8,568	13,200	13,200	13,200	13,200	13,200	13,200	13,200
School meals	0	0	0	252	1,278	1,278	1,278	1,278	1,278	1,278
Food at home	2,307	4,707	7,107	8,799	8,799	8,799	8,799	8,799	8,799	8,799
Cell phone	0	0	0	420	420	420	420	420	420	420
Utilities	2,070	2,070	2,070	2,070	2,400	2,400	2,400	2,400	2,400	2,400
Net income	7,350	13,428	15,045	11,611	14,513	20,100	25,554	31,683	37,868	42,375

The following graph depicts the increases and decreases in net income (i.e., cash income) as gross pay increases in the preceding table.

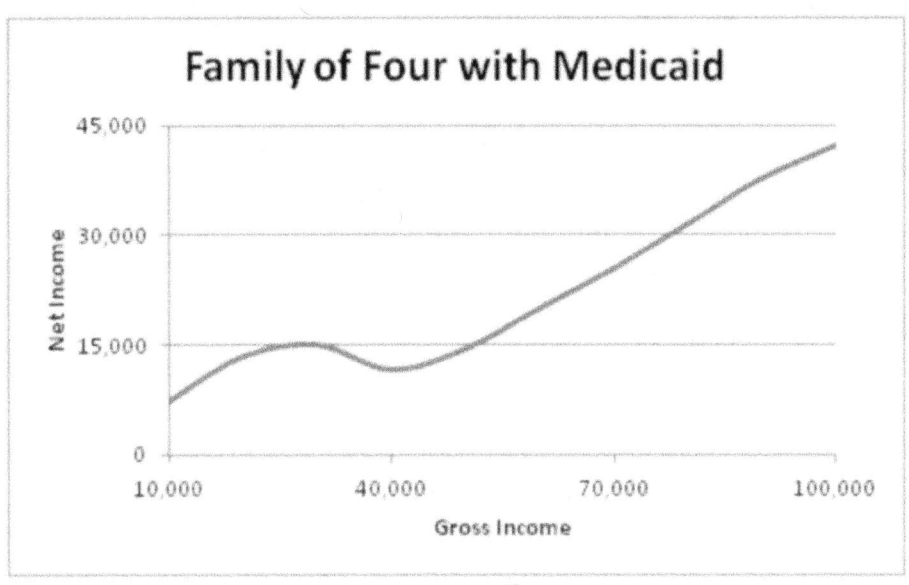

The following table and graph show the net income of a family of three (a single adult and two children) assuming expanded Medicaid.

Net Income for a Family of Three with ACA Medicaid Expansion										
Gross pay	10,000	20,000	30,000	40,000	50,000	60,000	70,000	80,000	90,000	100,000
FICA	765	1,530	2,295	3,060	3,825	4,590	5,355	6,120	6,885	7,650
Federal income tax	0	0	938	2,269	3,769	5,269	6,846	9,346	11,846	14,346
EIC & child credit	-5,060	-6,847	-4,741	-2,635	-2,000	-2,000	-2,000	-1,750	-1,250	-750
State tax	0	292	883	1,483	2,083	2,683	3,283	3,883	4,483	5,083
Net after tax	14,295	25,025	30,625	35,823	42,323	49,458	56,516	62,401	68,036	73,671
Health Care	0	0	6,382	6,382	6,382	6,382	6,382	6,382	6,382	6,382
ACA Credit	0	0	5,782	4,416	3,016	1,468	0	0	0	0
Net after ACA	14,295	25,025	30,025	33,857	38,957	44,544	50,134	56,019	61,654	67,289
Housing Rent	2,712	5,712	8,712	13,200	13,200	13,200	13,200	13,200	13,200	13,200
School meals	0	0	252	1,278	1,278	1,278	1,278	1,278	1,278	1,278
Food at home	1,403	3,815	6,599	6,599	6,599	6,599	6,599	6,599	6,599	6,599
Cell phone	0	0	420	420	420	420	420	420	420	420
Utilities	2,070	2,070	2,070	2,400	2,400	2,400	2,400	2,400	2,400	2,400
Net income		8,110	13,428	11,972	9,960	15,060	20,647	26,237	32,122	37,757	43,392

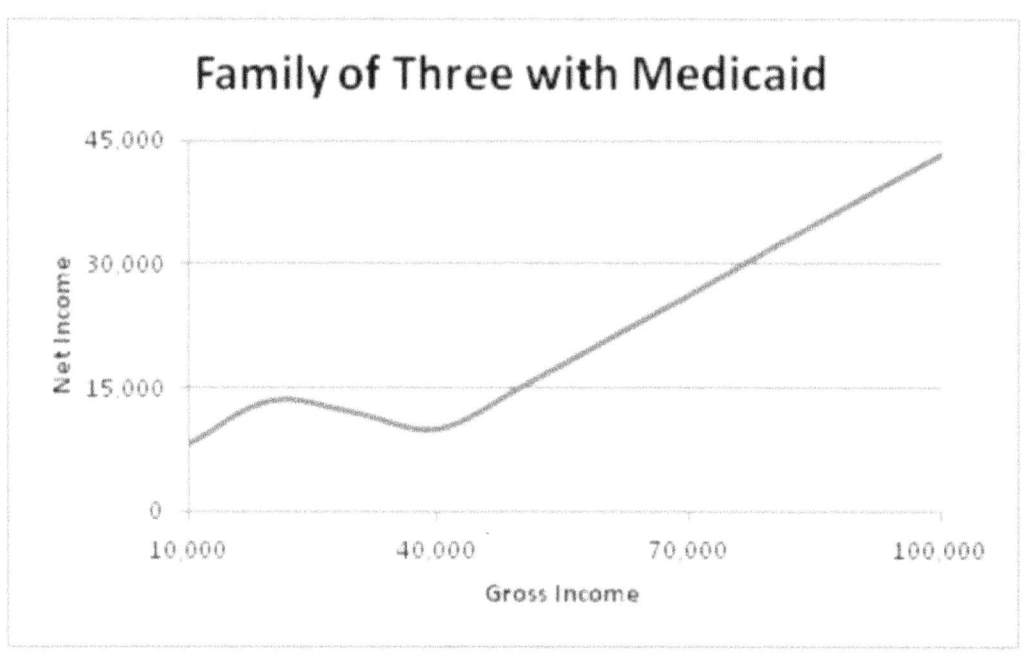

Family of Three with Medicaid

Georgia's income tax system is used in both of the above charts because it is somewhat "run of the mill" in terms of state income tax systems. The highest rate is 6 percent. (Some states do not have a state income tax.) The tax credits and entitlements are those commonly available to lower-income and lower-middle-income persons. They are thoroughly described in Chapter 7. Although many other less common credits and entitlements potentially apply, they are not considered. However, they would have little impact on the results. "EIC" stands for the earned income tax credit, and "child credit" stands for the child care credit. Gross rental costs of $1,100 per month are the assumed. The costs shown are net of Section 8 housing (if applicable). Health Care and the ACA credit relate to Obamacare health insurance purchased on an Obamacare exchange. Obamacare coverage applies when an individual acquires coverage through an Obamacare exchange. As discussed in Chapter 7, employees receiving affordable coverage from their employer generally are not eligible for Obamacare and related tax credits.

Georgia has not expanded Medicaid in connection with Obamacare. How does a failure to expand Medicaid coverage impact the equation? The answer is: not much. However, a small segment of the population would switch from (essentially free) Medicaid health care to whatever the state offers in terms of Medicaid and non-Medicaid coverage for lower-income persons. States that have not expanded Medicaid coverage differ in terms of when Medicaid is available. According to the Centers for Medicare and Medicaid Services (CMS), Maine grants Medicaid to families with income at or below 100 percent of the FPL. Like many other states that have not expanded Medicaid to 138 percent of the FPL, Georgia has a complex system for Medicaid. It is described in Chapter 7. Most states have beneficial coverage for children, in part funded by the federal State

Children's Health Insurance Program (SCHIP). Practically, for the vast majority of persons whose income is near or below the FPL, they will not pay for health care coverage. State laws may exempt their income from garnishment. Also, it is financially impractical (and imprudent) to pay significant legal fees to obtain an unenforceable judgment. Thus, providers often will not pursue collection. Of course, some providers may refuse to provide services. Federal law prohibits hospitals from denying emergency services. The following chart assumes that such persons will not pay for coverage for any family member. It is the cash flow breakdown for a family of four, assuming the state tax system is the same as Georgia's tax system and there is no Obamacare expansion of Medicaid.

Net Income for a Family of Four with No ACA Medicaid Expansion									
Gross pay	10,000	20,000	30,000	40,000	50,000	60,000	70,000	80,000	90,000	100,000
FICA	765	1,530	2,295	3,060	3,825	4,590	5,355	6,120	6,885	7,650
Federal income tax	0	0	221	1,223	2,441	3,941	5,441	6,941	8,441	9,941
EIC & child credit	-5,060	-7,372	-5,865	-3,759	-2,000	-2,000	-2,000	-2,000	-2,000	-2,000
State tax	0	69	559	1,159	1,759	2,359	2,959	3,559	4,159	4,759
Net after tax	14,295	25,773	32,790	38,317	43,975	51,110	58,245	65,380	72,515	79,650
Health Care	0	0	11,178	11,178	11,178	11,178	11,178	11,178	11,178	11,178
ACA Credit	0	0	10,578	9,213	7,813	6,265	4,584	3,578	2,628	0
Net after ACA	14,295	25,773	32,190	36,352	40,610	46,197	51,651	57,780	63,965	68,472
Housing Rent	2,568	5,568	8,568	13,200	13,200	13,200	13,200	13,200	13,200	13,200
School meals	0	0	0	252	1,278	1,278	1,278	1,278	1,278	1,278
Food at home	2,307	4,707	7,107	8,799	8,799	8,799	8,799	8,799	8,799	8,799
Cell phone	0	0	0	420	420	420	420	420	420	420
Utilities	2,070	2,070	2,070	2,070	2,400	2,400	2,400	2,400	2,400	2,400
Net income	7,350	13,428	14,445	11,611	14,513	20,100	25,554	31,683	37,868	42,375

The following graph depicts the increases and decreases in net income as gross pay increases.

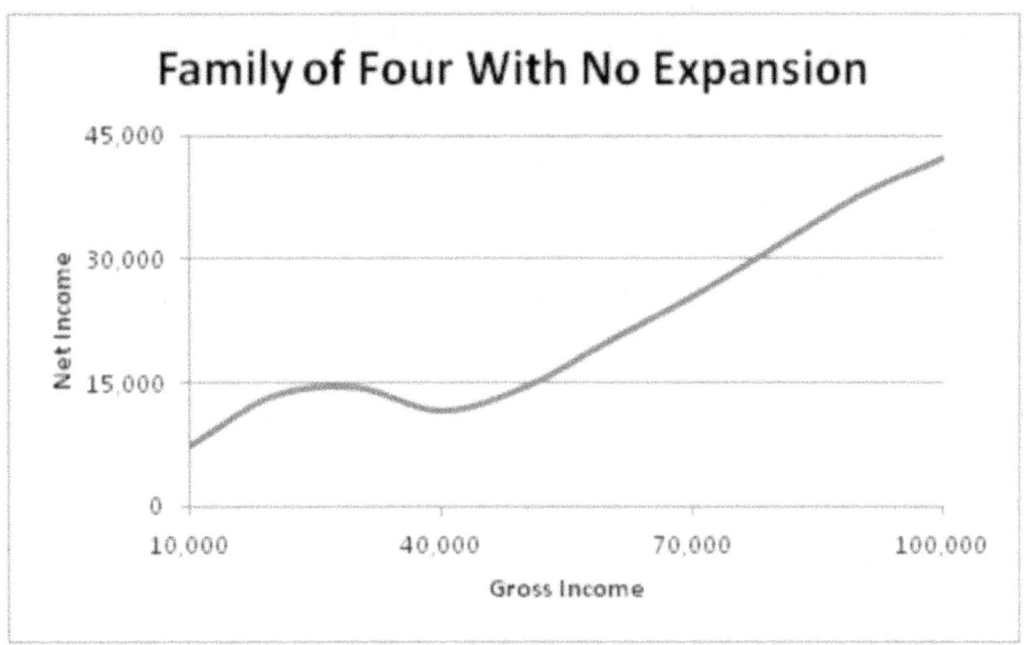

Because of deductibles, co-insurance, and other factors involving private insurance coverage, Medicaid is less expensive than private coverage with Obamacare premium tax credits on a net basis. Many employees now receive health care coverage from their employer on a tax-free basis. The following table is the same as the first table above, but it assumes that affordable Obamacare-compliant employer coverage is provided at no cost to employed persons who are not eligible for Medicaid coverage:

Net Income for a Family of Four with Employer Coverage									
Gross pay	10,000	20,000	30,000	40,000	50,000	60,000	70,000	80,000	90,000	100,000
FICA	765	1,530	2,295	3,060	3,825	4,590	5,355	6,120	6,885	7,650
Federal income tax	0	0	221	1,223	2,441	3,941	5,441	6,941	8,441	9,941
EIC & child credit	-5,060	-7,372	-5,865	-3,759	-2,000	-2,000	-2,000	-2,000	-2,000	-2,000
State tax	0	69	559	1,159	1,759	2,359	2,959	3,559	4,159	4,759
Net after tax	14,295	25,773	32,790	38,317	43,975	51,110	58,245	65,380	72,515	79,650
Health Care	0	0	0	0	0	0	0	0	0	0
ACA Credit	0	0	0	0	0	0	0	0	0	0
Net after ACA	14,295	25,773	32,790	38,317	43,975	51,110	58,245	65,380	72,515	79,650
Housing Rent	2,568	5,568	8,568	13,200	13,200	13,200	13,200	13,200	13,200	13,200
School meals	0	0	0	252	1,278	1,278	1,278	1,278	1,278	1,278
Food at home	2,307	4,707	7,107	8,799	8,799	8,799	8,799	8,799	8,799	8,799
Cell phone	0	0	0	420	420	420	420	420	420	420
Utilities	2,070	2,070	2,070	2,070	2,400	2,400	2,400	2,400	2,400	2,400
Net income	7,350	13,428	15,045	13,576	17,878	25,013	32,148	39,283	46,418	53,553

The following graph depicts the increases and decreases in net income as gross pay in the previous table increases.

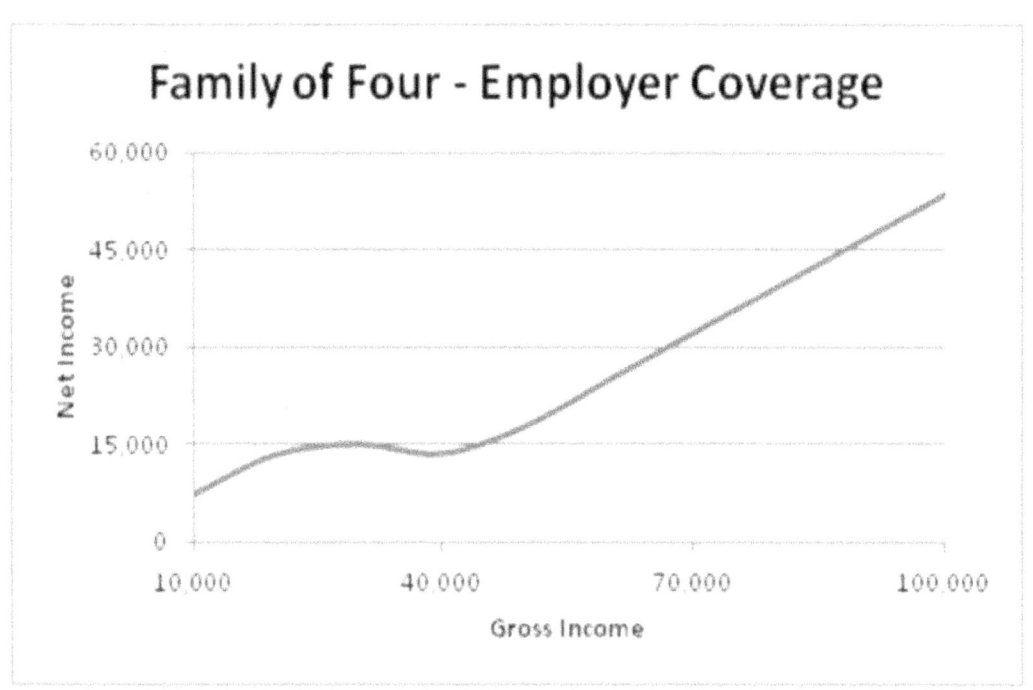

In the above materials, Section 8 housing is deemed to end once income exceeds $30,000 because the rental amount ($1,100) is relatively low. However, it could still be available to a person or household with an income that exceeds $50,000. Also, it might not be available to a person or household whose income is $30,000 or less. This is so because of the complex way in which Section 8 housing works. Section 8 housing is very sensitive to income changes and local income averages. Summaries of how Section 8 and the rest of the common entitlements work (in terms of eligibility) are supplied in Chapter 7.

Returning to the Ditch. It should be obvious from the preceding cash flow charts and graphs that lifestyle actually diminishes once a family's income exceeds the higher end of the low-income range (approximately $30,000 for a family of four) and enters the lower end of the middle-income range. This is so primarily because entitlements phase out, and it takes roughly $20,000 of supplemental income for the lifestyle of a family of four to increase once one enters "the ditch." The problem is, very few people or families who make approximately $30,000 per year can make a $20,000+ income move in a year or even a few years. So, why try? Why not lay low and keep income below the entitlements phase-out? The system encourages one to stay put.

So, as this book is titled, why work? When you are on the cusp of entering the ditch, why work overtime or take a promotion to produce more cash flow, when the net result will be a decline in one's standard of living? Unless extra work is deemed beneficial from a health perspective or for some other reason, one would be foolish to work more and incur a standard of living reduction. *The ditch is a national disgrace!*

According to a December 9, 2013, report by CBS News entitled "Americans' net worth hits all-time high," the median household income in October of 2013 was $52,299. According to the U.S. Census Bureau, for 2011, approximately 25 percent of U.S. households had income below $25,000 and approximately 25 percent of households had income between $25,000 and $50,000. Wages and salaries have not changed much since then. Accordingly, a significant percentage of the American population falls within the ditch. It is likely that many do not realize they would be better off with less income.

A large percentage of American households (i.e., 35-40 percent) have income between $15,000 and $50,000 per year. These households experience roughly the same standard of living. And, many households with income between $29,000 and $50,000 have a lower standard of living than households with income of $15,000 to $29,000. So, semi-socialism applies to a large segment of the U.S. population.

Whatever the policy should be regarding safety nets and entitlements, it clearly is not fair and not good policy for the ditch to exist. Lifestyle should always only improve as income increases. Significant changes are needed.

The entitlements and tax credits resulting in the ditch are the earned income tax credit, Obamacare, Medicaid, Section 8 housing, food stamps, free and reduced school lunches and breakfasts, low-income utilities help, and free cell phones. Other entitlements and tax credits exist that could potentially impact the ditch. Common entitlements and credits are outlined in Chapter 7.

Just as the mentioned entitlements create the ditch and thereby create a disincentive to advance, federal financial aid for college and nursing home entitlements destroy the incentive for people to make money and save. Simply put, the more you make and the more you have, the more you'll pay for your children's college and nursing home care.

Federal Financial Aid. Federal financial aid for college is provided in the form of various grants and loans. For a family situation where the child is dependent, net worth and earnings determine the Expected Family Contribution, or "EFC." The EFC is the amount the family must pay towards college. The balance is provided by government grants (including the Pell grant), institutional grants and loans. The main source is grants.

A lengthy form called the Free Application for Federal Student Aid (FAFSA) must be completed and filed to determine the EFC. The main source of information is the parent's or parents' most recent federal income tax return. Basically, taxable income is adjusted by a few additions and subtractions, added to 12 percent of a portion of the family's net worth, multiplied by a factor and then divided by the number of children in college to produce the EFC. One of the adjustments to income is that 401(k) and IRA contributions must be added back.

Income includes nontaxable income. Investments include cash, CDs, stocks, bonds, net equity in real estate, and Section 529 plan assets. *The home is exempt, as are all retirement savings.* As discussed below, the value of an interest in a small business is also exempt. A dollar amount exemption applies to investments. The exemption amount depends on whether there are one or two parents and the age of the oldest parent (or, for a one-parent family, the age of the parent). For example, if the oldest parent of a two-parent family will be age 54 on December 31, 2014, the investment exemption amount is $38,500.

For individuals falling in certain lower-income levels, the EFC is $0. For example, for families who participate in the free or reduced lunch program with an income of $24,000 or less, the EFC is $0.

The 2014–2015 EFC formula for a dependent student follows.

2014–2015 EFC FORMULA A : DEPENDENT STUDENT

PARENTS' INCOME IN 2013

1. Parents' Adjusted Gross Income (FAFSA/SAR #85) If negative, enter zero.	
2. a. Parent 1 (father/mother/stepparent) income earned from work (FAFSA/SAR #88)	
2. b. Parent 2 (father/mother/stepparent) income earned from work (FAFSA/SAR #89) +	
Total parents' income earned from work =	
3. Parents' Taxable Income (If tax filers, enter the amount from line 1 above. If non-tax filers, enter the amount from line 2.)*	
4. Total untaxed income and benefits (Total of FAFSA/SAR #94a. through 94i.) +	
5. Taxable and untaxed income (sum of line 3 and line 4) =	
6. Total additional financial information (Total of FAFSA/SAR #93a. through 93f.) –	
7. TOTAL INCOME (line 5 minus line 6) May be a negative number. =	

ALLOWANCES AGAINST PARENTS' INCOME

8. 2013 U.S. income tax paid (FAFSA/SAR #86) (tax filers only) If negative, enter zero.	
9. State and other tax allowance (Table A1) If negative, enter zero. +	
10. Parent 1 (father/mother/stepparent) Social Security tax allowance (Table A2) +	
11. Parent 2 (father/mother/stepparent) Social Security tax allowance (Table A2) +	
12. Income protection allowance (Table A3) +	
13. Employment expense allowance: • Two working parents (Parents' Marital Status is "married" or "unmarried and both parents living together"): 35% of the lesser of the earned incomes, or $4,000, whichever is less • One-parent families: 35% of earned income, or $4,000, whichever is less • Two-parent families, one working parent: enter zero. +	
14. TOTAL ALLOWANCES =	

*STOP HERE if the following are true:

Line 3 is $24,000 or less **and**

• The parents are eligible to file a 2013 IRS Form 1040A or 1040EZ (they are not required to file a 2013 Form 1040) or they are not required to file any income tax return **or**
• Anyone included in the parents' household size (as defined on the FAFSA) received benefits during 2012 or 2013 from any of the designated means-tested federal benefit programs **or**
• Either of the parents is a dislocated worker.

If these circumstances are true, the Expected Family Contribution is automatically zero.

AVAILABLE INCOME

Total income (from line 7)	
Total allowances (from line 14) –	
15. AVAILABLE INCOME (AI) May be a negative number. =	

PARENTS' CONTRIBUTION FROM ASSETS

16. Cash, savings & checking (FAFSA/SAR #90)		
17. Net worth of investments** (FAFSA/SAR #91) If negative, enter zero.		
18. Net worth of business and/or investment farm (FAFSA/SAR #92) If negative, enter zero.		
19. Adjusted net worth of business/farm (Calculate using Table A4.) +		
20. Net worth (sum of lines 16, 17, and 19) =		
21. Education savings and asset protection allowance (Table A5) –		
22. Discretionary net worth (line 20 minus line 21) =		
23. Asset conversion rate ×		.12
24. CONTRIBUTION FROM ASSETS If negative, enter zero. =		

PARENTS' CONTRIBUTION

AVAILABLE INCOME (AI) (from line 15)	
CONTRIBUTION FROM ASSETS (from line 24) +	
25. Adjusted Available Income (AAI) May be a negative number. =	
26. Total parents' contribution from AAI (Calculate using Table A6.) If negative, enter zero.	
27. Number in college in 2014–2015 (Exclude parents) (FAFSA/SAR #74) ÷	
28. PARENTS' CONTRIBUTION (standard contribution for nine-month enrollment)*** If negative, enter zero. =	

**Do *not* include the family's home.

*** To calculate the parents' contribution for other than nine-month enrollment, see page 11.

continued on the next page

42

Returning to Diane's aggravation with her close friend's much easier lifestyle, federal financial aid for college was the great equalizer. The mistakes that she and her husband made compared to her friend who ate out regularly and took luxurious vacations were: (a) they saved instead of spending their excess cash flow each year, and (b) their children were born more than three years apart instead of one year apart.

Based on assumed ownership of the $175,000 rental house, CDs of $40,000, annual income averaging $110,000, no "above the line" tax deductions and $20,000 of itemized deductions for each year that the children were in college, the total amount she and her husband would have paid to educate their children for all years of college would have been approximately $232,856. This figure is the net of the American Opportunity Tax Credit for each year (described in Chapter 7). In contrast, the total amount that her easygoing friend and her husband would have paid for their children's higher education (net of tax credits) would have been approximately $55,782. (All of the income and deduction figures described above are assumed to apply to Diane's friend and her husband.) Thus, the total that Diane and her husband would have paid for college for her two children would have been $177,074 more than the total that Diane's friend and her husband spent. This difference ($177,074) equals 82 percent of the $215,000 that Diane and her husband saved in the form of CDs and a rental house, thus explaining how Diane's friend and her husband could live a relatively luxurious lifestyle while having basically the same net income as Diane and her husband.

Standing alone, saving instead of spending excess cash on hand each year cost Diane and her husband $79,640 for all years, compared to what they would have paid had they not saved. This figure is 37 percent of the assets saved of $215,000. The balance of the difference is attributable to the years their children were born apart. Tax credits aside, having their children more than three years apart instead of having them one year a part cost Diane and her husband the balance of $97,434.

Unfortunately, few people consider federal financial aid for college when having children. Generally, people have children without evaluating the impact of college costs or government aid.

Let's analyze the logic (or lack thereof) of dividing the amount that must be paid by the number of children in college. In terms of income, it is logical that having to pay two college tuitions (and other college costs) in one year instead of having to pay one would be much more burdensome for all but relatively wealthy individuals. Yet, should it be enough to cause the $97,434 differential, given that the only difference is that one woman had her children one year apart and the other woman had her children four years apart? Savings is usually produced over a relatively long period of time. As the above example hopefully evidences, it is completely unfair to divide savings by the number of children in college.

For many families, a substantial amount of accumulated wealth will be lost during the college years due to payment of college costs. While many families may be able to make up the lost wealth, often, the parents are in their mid-50s when the wealth is lost, thus making it hard to recover before attaining retirement age.

Nursing Home Care. Many people accumulate significant assets by the time they retire. Most elderly people either don't or can't work. Thus, they ordinarily "spend down" their accumulated assets in their retirement years. For most people, their personal assets are supplemented by Social Security benefits. Also, Medicare pays much of the medical costs of the elderly. While Medicare is entirely a federal government program, Medicaid is funded by both the federal and state governments. For the most part, Medicaid is administered by the states.

Nursing home care is, absent financial need, a personal expense. However, similar to federal financial aid for college, Medicaid will provide for nursing home costs to the extent there is financial need. State law generally provides for estate recovery of the costs paid by the state following death, but exceptions and exemptions reduce the recovery amount that must be paid. Furthermore, at least in Georgia, interest is not charged with respect to the amount owed to the state following death.

In Georgia, the average monthly cost of a nursing home in 2014 is approximately $6,000 per month. Thus, the ordinary annual cost for someone to pay the tab out-of-pocket would be in the $72,000 range. The state pays a lower cost than what a private citizen must pay.

To be eligible for nursing home care in Georgia (as is the case in other states), an individual must pass an income test and an asset test. Generally speaking, in Georgia, if an individual's income is 300 percent of the federal Supplemental Security Income (SSI) figure for the year or less, the individual passes the income test. For 2014, the SSI figure for a single person is $721. (SSI supplies supplemental income to certain individuals whose income falls below the SSI minimum necessary cash income figure.)

Thus, if an individual's monthly income is less than $2,163, he or she passes the income test.

For individuals with income in excess of 300 percent of SSI, it is generally still possible to qualify for state-subsidized nursing home care if income is run through a Medicaid Qualifying Income Trust (i.e., a "Miller trust"). With a Miller trust, an individual can use the income from the trust to pay personal needs, needs of the individual's spouse (if married), needs of dependent children (if applicable), non-Medicaid covered health costs, health insurance premiums and the patient's share of the nursing home cost (which generally is the remainder after all of the preceding costs have been taken into account). The amount that can be paid to a spouse can be substantial. For 2014, it is the amount necessary to increase the spouse's income to $2,931.

The general asset limit to qualify for nursing home care is $2,000. However, many assets are exempt from the limit. Also, for married individuals, the limit is much higher ($117,240 in 2014) because the spouse's needs are considered.

Exempt assets include the entire value of a home for married persons. For single persons in Georgia, up to $543,000 of home equity is exempt in 2014. While retirement accounts generally are considered assets, they are exempt if paid out as an annuity or if paid pursuant to the minimum distribution guidelines of Internal Revenue Code Section 401(a)(9). A life annuity from a pension plan would be exempt. Household goods generally are exempt. The value of one vehicle generally is exempt. Certain amounts set aside for death, including the costs of a burial plot and a gravesite, are exempt.

Generally speaking, an individual's assets given away five or more years before seeking nursing home entry are excluded from the assets calculation. To the extent the five-year period has not been exhausted, a penalty applies. The penalty is the individual must pay for care for the number of months produced by dividing the amount of assets given away during the five-year period by the average cost of nursing home care in the state.

As noted, exceptions and exemptions exist to estate recovery by the state. In Georgia, recovery is supposed to take place only against the patient's estate. Ordinarily, in legal terminology, an individual's estate would mean his probate estate. However, the State of Georgia has attempted to include non-probate type assets, such as retirement plan benefits, in this definition. Georgia will not pursue a home with less than $25,000 of equity. Furthermore, if a spouse or dependent resides in the home after the death of the patient, there won't be any recovery against the home until it is no longer occupied by the spouse or dependent.

It should be clear that it is possible to plan to avoid or minimize the costs of a nursing home, just as it is possible to plan to prevent one's self from having too much income to qualify for day-to-day entitlements or to prevent one's personal circumstances from resulting in costly college costs. But, with two possible exceptions, people don't live their lives with these entitlement rules as their decision drivers. Certainly, many lower-income persons know where or roughly where the lines are drawn in terms of entitlements eligibility. Wealthy persons can also know the rules and plan accordingly. But, the average Joe who is middle class or perhaps upper middle class is unaware of how these entitlements impact his economic well-being (i.e., living standard).

Roughly the Same Place. So, how did the four women end up in the same place, and what were their financial conditions immediately prior to entering the nursing home?

Tracy received all of the federal entitlements available while she raised her children and thereafter. These entitlements include Section 8 housing, Medicaid, WIC, food stamps (SNAP), reduced and free school lunches, LIHEAP (utilities), and Lifeline (free cell phone). With Section 8 housing, she was able to rent a house in the Wee-Land Homes subdivision for less than 30 percent of the ordinary rental amount. She paid nothing toward the college education of her children. Her nursing home care is provided for by the state.

Barbie will need to lose all but $2,000 of the $10,000 of cash she has accumulated to cover her nursing home care. She will need to take her retirement benefits in installments to exempt them from her nursing home cost share. If she doesn't pay a planner (or find someone to help her for free) to advise her on how to protect her retirement assets, she will need to pay her retirement benefits to herself (with potential tax consequences) and use them to pay for her nursing home care until her cash runs out. Her lifetime average income was slightly beyond the entitlements threshold, resulting in little or no aid to her family. However, most of the costs of her children's education would have been covered by the federal government or through loans. Assuming their income was $60,000 and their cash and investments averaged $10,000 for each year that their children were in college, she and her husband would have paid approximately $15,316 for the college education of her two children for all years of college attended. This figure is net of the benefit of the American Opportunity Tax Credit for each year. For the reasons noted in the charts and graphs regarding entitlements and taxes, the difference in lifestyle between Barbie and Tracy would have been negligible. Tracy might have had a higher standard of living than Barbie for some or perhaps even most of her lifetime.

Diane would have experienced a slightly higher standard of living than Barbie and Tracy. However, most of the accumulated wealth of her and her husband would have been lost over the years that they paid for their children's education. In other words, wealth accumulated until Diane's children attended college would have been largely consumed to pay for the college costs of her children. With the exception of the value in her home, what was left would have been consumed to pay for the nursing home to the tune of approximately $6,000 per month. If the state funded part of Diane's nursing home care, the equity in the home would be taken by the state following Diane's death to the extent necessary to make the state whole. However, as further discussed below, had she and her husband planned for the possibility of nursing home care needs, she could have received the care for little or no cost.

According to the U.S. Department of Health and Human Services, National Clearinghouse for Long Term Care Information, *What Does Long Term Care Cost?*, the average nursing home stay for a woman is 3.7 years. Absent effective planning, assuming a 3.7 year stay for Diane, most of Diane's wealth would have been consumed to pay for her nursing home care.

Eleanor's lifestyle would have been better than the lifestyles of Tracy, Barbie, and Diane. However, she would not have qualified for nursing home care, thus costing her approximately $72,000 per year. Further, a significant portion of the wealth accumulated by her and her husband at the time their children attended college would have been consumed at that time. In this regard, Eleanor and her husband would have paid approximately $400,000 for the four-year college education of her two children (i.e., the full cost). Thus, by the time her children finished college, a lot of the wealth that she and her husband had accumulated would have been consumed. She and her husband built new wealth after their children left college. As discussed below, had Eleanor taken steps to better plan for her old age, she could have possibly received her nursing home care for free.

The annual tax payments by the four women (and, with the exception of Tracy, their spouses) are important to note. Tracy would have paid no federal income taxes in any year. She would have paid FICA tax, but it would have been greatly exceeded by the refundable tax credits to which she was entitled. So, on a net basis, she paid nothing and annually received approximately $24,000 of cash and benefits from the federal government. She would have paid less than $300 of Georgia income tax each year. Barbie and her husband would have averaged $4,000-$5,000 of federal tax liability each year and $1,500-$2,000 of state income tax liability. Diane and her husband would have annually paid approximately $16,000 in federal income and FICA taxes and $5,000 in Georgia income tax. Assuming $40,000 of itemized deductions, $150,000 of salary and $100,000 of profits allocations from Frank Fixes It, Eleanor and her husband would have paid approximately $60,000 per year in federal income and FICA taxes and approximately $7,000 per year in Georgia income taxes.

In the following chapter, means of planning to maximize entitlements and minimize taxes are discussed.

Chapter 5

Federally Favored Activities and Planning

Hopefully from the discussion so far, it is apparent that the current federal system of entitlements and taxation clearly favors certain activities. A discussion of favored activities follows. It should be noted that these activities are currently favored by federal law, but federal law can and will change in pertinent respects.

Retirement Benefits. Perhaps the most favored activity is saving for retirement through tax-qualified retirement plans and IRAs. The benefits include:

- An income tax deduction for contributions

- Potential tax credits for lower-income contributors

- Tax-free growth

- Assets excluded from the federal financial aid calculations

- Assets generally protected from creditors in the event of bankruptcy

- Assets excluded from SNAP eligibility calculations

- Assets generally protected from IRS collection activities

- Assets can be converted to an annuity to minimize or eliminate nursing home costs

- Distributions generally not required until age 70½ (later for most employed persons with respect to their employers' plans; not required for Roth IRAs)

Thus, to the extent an individual can do so, he or she should take advantage of tax-qualified plans and IRA benefits. Following termination of employment, tax-qualified benefits can be "rolled over" tax-free to IRAs by individuals, thus permitting continued tax-free growth.

It should be noted that the Obama Administration now appears to be targeting retirement plans. The 2014 State of the Union address of President Obama provided evidence of this aim.

There are many cases where, on a tax-deductible basis, tax-qualified plans can provide significantly greater benefits to highly paid employees than those provided to non-highly paid employees of the same company. Professional firms, such as law firms, use "cross-tested" plans to provide very substantial tax-deductible benefits for highly paid professionals relative to the benefits provided to staff employees. In some cases, potentially hundreds of thousands of dollars can be "put away" for a highly paid employee in one year in the form of tax-deductible contributions to one or more tax-qualified retirement plans. Such arrangements are completely lawful. It would seem reasonable for greater limits to be placed on these arrangements by Congress.

Owning a Home. Owning a home produces many benefits. Included in the benefits are:

- Tax deductions for home mortgage interest

- Tax-free gain upon most sales

- Exclusion from the federal financial aid calculations

- Exclusion from SNAP eligibility calculations

- General exemption from IRS collection activities, and reachable by creditors in bankruptcy to only a limited degree

- General exemption from Medicaid nursing home calculations while living

Certain Work. *With the very important exception of people who are at the upper end of the lower-income scale and people who have children in college*, work generally is favored. Generally, cash flow increases as cash income from work increases. The earned income tax credit is available only to workers who earn money. And work, or attempted work, generally is necessary for the nonelderly to receive food stamps. However, for persons whose income level is on the front cusp of the ditch, work and the pay it brings can actually diminish one's standard of living. For people with children in college, greater income means a greater EFC.

Being in Need. It should be obvious that a tremendous amount of benefits are provided for people who are in need. As need decreases, entitlements decrease. As shown in the tables in Chapter 4, one's lifestyle can diminish significantly due to loss of entitlements. Thus, the current system creates incentives for a large part of the population to "lay low" and stay in the income range that qualifies for the entitlements.

Debt. The U.S. system favors debt. Mortgage debt interest is tax-deductible for income tax purposes. Interest on a HELOC is also tax deductible. As the Federal Reserve Bank "buys bonds," it is printing money, thereby decreasing the value of each existing dollar. If one is a debtor and the value of the dollar decreases, real debt diminishes. Finally, debts reduce net worth, and net worth generally is a significant factor in determining federal financial aid and entitlement to Medicaid.

Having Children. Growing family size increases the amount of household income that can be received without losing eligibility for entitlements.   The more children a family has, the more of certain entitlements the family is entitled to receive (e.g., food stamps).   A tax deduction (i.e., a personal exemption) is permitted for each child.   Tax credits exist for each child, as well as for college costs of children. Minimizing the age differences between children maximizes the federal financial aid a family can receive.

Health Care. Generally speaking, health care provided by an employer is tax free to the employee. Self-employed persons, including partners in service partnerships and LLCs, can deduct the full cost of health insurance for income tax purposes. Also, if the coverage qualifies as a high deductible health plan described in Internal Revenue Code Section 223, then a health savings account (HSA) can be maintained that provides for tax-deductible contributions to it, tax-free growth of assets, and tax-free distributions as long as the distributions are used to pay for health care. The 2014 contribution limits for HSAs are $3,300 for single coverage and $6,550 for family coverage.

Gifting, Including Charitable Gifting. Gifts reduce net worth, and net worth is a determining factor for many entitlements, including federal financial aid for college and nursing home care. Charitable gifts ordinarily are tax deductible.

Planning. Based on the list of favored activities, it is possible to plan the best course of action if the facts allow choices to be made.

For those with children who can pull it off, maximizing retirement plan assets and home value while minimizing other investments and income while children are in college is an absolute winner. The retirement assets and home value would be excluded from the college assets analysis. If income is low, the EFC would ordinarily be low. The question is: How many can pull it off? Imagine a person who has been slowly advancing in his or her career for decades. With few exceptions, putting on the brakes for a few years is unrealistic and would ordinarily be detrimental in the long run.

For example, consider a husband and wife who have $70,000 of Adjusted Gross Income (AGI) who can, but have not, contributed money to an IRA or tax-qualified 401(k) plan. The couple was planning on investing $10,000 in a five-year CD. Assume the couple has $90,000 in investments and a 15-year old child (their only child) who will enter college in a few years. Contributing $10,000 to a tax-qualified plan or IRA would reduce their AGI to $60,000, thereby reducing federal and state income tax by $2,100 ($1,500 being federal), increasing Obamacare credits by $1,468 and allowing them to receive $200 in saver's tax credits. Furthermore, the $10,000 reduction in net worth would reduce their college costs for four years by $2,256 (i.e., $10,000 x .12 x.47 x 4). The combined savings would mean their net out-of-pocket cost would be $3,976. They'll also have "put away" $10,000 for retirement, and that investment will grow tax free and very likely will be tax free upon withdrawal in retirement.

If one is on the upper cusp of the lower-income threshold for most of the significant entitlements and is receiving all the major entitlements, such as Section 8 housing, he or she should think twice before working more hours or taking a promotion. An individual may significantly regret working more or taking a promotion if the value of entitlements lost exceeds the net cash flow produced by the additional work or promotion.

There is a limited exemption for Section 529 assets and other investments when it comes to calculating federal financial aid for college. However, retirement assets are fully exempt from the equation. If possible, individuals should skip 529 contributions and deposit the money in a retirement plan or IRA. The contribution would ordinarily produce a tax deduction. Traditionally, retirement distributions have ordinarily been subjected to lower tax rates in retirement than the rates applicable when earned. However, as discussed below, the growing federal debt and entitlements situation could cause this traditional pattern to change. (A section 529 plan provides for tax-free growth of assets and tax-free distributions of accumulated funds that are used for certain college costs. Income taxation and a 10 percent excise tax apply to earnings not used for permissible college costs.)

The Section 529 assets of grandparents are not part of the federal financial aid equation. Thus, where possible, have a grandparent establish a 529 account instead of a parent or child.

With real estate prices being depressed and interest rates low, many have opted to buy rental property. Tax deductions exist for mortgage interest and depreciation. However, given all of the foregoing considerations, one should query whether it would better to instead maximize retirement contributions (if not already maximized). If an IRA exists, a real estate investment could be made through it, including property partially funded by debt. Debt-financed income could potentially produce unrelated taxable business income, but deductions often exceed rental income, thus meaning no income tax liability. However, the prohibited transaction rules are of concern when investing through an IRA. These rules generally prohibit transactions between an IRA owner and the IRA's property. For example, personal use of real estate owned by an IRA would be a prohibited transaction. If a prohibited transaction occurs, all of the IRA's assets are deemed distributed (in a taxable transaction) on the first day of the year in which the prohibited transaction occurred. Thereafter, there is no IRA.

For people who are aging and have a child or relative they trust to help them in the event of need, gifting assets well in advance of the potential need for nursing home care ordinarily is a prudent financial move. The federal estate and gift tax exemption is now large enough ($5,340,000) that few people need to be concerned about estate and gift taxes. Also, increasing the value of one's home instead of purchasing investments can help one's stance in terms of both federal financial aid and nursing home care. Finally, receiving tax-qualified plan assets in the form of an annuity [or receiving income for life or minimum required distributions as specified in Internal Revenue Code Section 401(a)(9)] can cause retirement plan assets to be exempt from Medicaid nursing home calculations.

For example, if a person has a home worth $400,000 that is subject to a $100,000 mortgage and also owns $80,000 of stocks, the person could sell the stocks and pay down the mortgage, thus allowing the person to immediately qualify for Medicaid nursing home coverage. Of course, if the stocks had appreciated in value, capital gain would exist upon their disposition.

When in doubt, if possible, people should buy a home. With the *general* exception of a bankruptcy situation, it is a well-protected asset. Mortgage payments produce tax deductions, and the home will be exempt from the federal financial aid equation and (generally) the nursing home equation. (However, generally, the equity in a home would be subject to estate recovery.) A home is exempt from food stamp assets eligibility calculations.

If a family with young teenagers or younger children owns significant investment assets and has been contemplating purchasing a larger home, the "upgrade" could help save on college costs. For example, a family with $150,000 of investments (e.g., stocks), $80,000 of Section 529 plan assets and two children born more than three years apart would save $8,460 for each year of college by using the $150,000 to upgrade (i.e., 150,000 x .12 x. 47). Of course, if the stocks had appreciated in value, long-term capital gain would exist on the sale. The highest potential federal tax rate attributable thereto is 20 percent. Higher earners could also be subject to the additional 3.8 percent tax on investment income.

Small businesses are excluded from the definition of "investments." For this purpose, a small business generally means a business with not more than 100 full-time or full-time equivalent employees that is owned and controlled by the family. If earnings have been distributed by the business on an annual basis (or roughly on an annual basis) and invested by the owner, the business could instead retain the earnings and invest them. The investment assets owned by the business should not be counted towards the investments total of the business owner for federal financial aid calculations purposes. Of course, there may be a concern about risk of loss due to the assets continuing to be held by the company. It *might* be possible to create a holding company to own the equity interests of the existing company, and have the existing company distribute the assets to the holding company (so that they would be safe from the operating company's creditors), without having the assets counted for federal financial aid purposes. It *might* also be lawful to make a capital contribution of assets to a company, thereby reducing personal assets taken into account for purposes of the federal financial aid calculations. Careful thought and analysis would be necessary to ensure legality and cost-effectiveness before undertaking any such planning actions.

For self-employed persons, there may be a means of reducing income just before a child enters or children enter college and continuing the lower income throughout the college years, thereby minimizing the EFC. In recent years, tremendous deductions have been permitted with respect to depreciation of capital assets, such as equipment and software. Many businesses have been able to "expense" (i.e., immediately deduct the full costs of) capital purchases. Certain retirement plans, such as a cash balance plan, can produce large tax-deductible contributions for highly paid individuals. Generally, a cash balance plan formula can be creative so as to provide for a relatively low allocation rate (e.g., 5 percent) for compensation up to a particular level (e.g., $50,000) and a high allocation rate with respect to compensation in excess thereof (e.g., 80 percent).

Certain demographics must exist in order for a cash balance plan to work. An option here might be making an S election for the business, purchasing capital assets (as needed), and establishing a cash balance plan to require significant contributions during the college years. The plan might be frozen thereafter. Reasonable compensation would need to be paid. The contributions to the cash balance plan would be tax deductible and would produce all of the previously discussed benefits of a retirement plan. Depending on the facts, it might be possible to "zero out" the taxable income of the company.

For example, imagine an LLC law firm owned and completely run by one married individual. (One of the co-authors has such a creature.) A single member LLC is a disregarded entity for federal tax purposes. In other words, it is deemed not to exist, and the LLC's net income must be reported by the owner on Schedule C of his or her income tax return. Assume the attorney is age 52 and averages net income of $175,000 per year (excluding any retirement expenses). Also, assume: (a) the attorney's spouse does not work; (b) the couple's deductible itemized deductions for interest, taxes and charitable contributions total $28,393; (c) the couple has a home and $100,000 of investments, $75,000 of which are Section 529 plan assets; (d) total college costs are $50,000 per year; and (e) net savings are invested in a Section 529 plan. Instead of the proposed course of action (i.e., investing net assets in a Section 529 plan), the attorney could make an S election for the business, pay himself or herself a reasonable salary (e.g., $100,000), and establish a cash balance pension plan with the following formula: 10 percent of the first $20,000 of compensation plus 80 percent of compensation in excess of $20,000. For a year when net income before deduction of compensation and pension contributions was $175,000, the required cash balance plan contribution would be $66,000 (i.e., 10 percent of $20,000 plus 80 percent of $80,000). The company's net income would be $1,350 [i.e., 175,000 – (100,000 + 66,000 + 7,650)]. ($7,650 is the company's FICA share.) If necessary to fund annual contributions, capital contributions could be made to the company. In lieu of doing nothing in terms of retirement benefit (i.e., instead investing in a 529 plan), this course of action would reduce federal income tax by $16,037 for each year. State income taxes would be reduced by $4,210. FICA and self-employment taxes would be reduced by $3,486. The total annual tax savings would be $23,733. Regarding federal financial aid for college, the annual savings would be $25,151. Adding the tax savings, the total annual savings would be $48,884. Applying these total savings for four years, the total saved

67

would be $195,536 (i.e., $48,884 x 4). While future distributions from the cash balance plan would be taxable, historically, most persons find themselves in a lower or much lower incremental tax bracket in retirement than the bracket they were in while working. The means of computing these figures is provided in the Appendix.

If borrowing is in order, special analysis is necessary. HELOC interest would be fully deductible, whereas interest with respect to an investment (e.g. a rental home) could be subject to limitations on income tax deductibility. However, a debt attributed to an investment ordinarily will reduce its value for both federal financial aid and nursing home calculation purposes.

For those who can do so, establishing an HSA with a high deductible health plan (HDHP) makes sense. The contributions to the HSA would be tax deductible. The health insurance premiums for the HDHP would be deductible for income tax purposes for a self-employed person. While not entirely clear from existing authorities, it is very likely that the HSA's assets would be excluded from the investments' total for purposes of federal financial aid for college and likely that the annual contributions would not have to be added back to income when calculating income for any year. A high deductible health plan is a plan that meets the requirement of Internal Revenue Code section 223(c)(2). Generally speaking, it provides for a minimum deductible ($1,250 for single coverage and $2,500 for family coverage for 2014) and places limits on maximum out-of-pocket costs for any given year ($6,350 for single coverage and $12,700 for family coverage for 2014).

Returning to Eleanor's situation, she has significant retirement assets ($800,000) in an IRA, $200,000 of stocks, and a home worth $750,000. Thus, she will not be eligible for free or state-subsidized nursing home care. The retirement assets likely were received from her husband's tax-qualified retirement plan upon his death. (They could have been housed in an IRA, instead of in a former employer plan.) Apparently, Eleanor's husband planned well to produce substantial tax-qualified plan retirement assets. However, he or she (or both of them) did not plan well for possible nursing home needs. Had Eleanor taken certain steps five or more years before needing nursing home care, she could have received the care for free. For example, had she (on a timely basis) gifted her stocks to her children or used them to fund an appropriately drafted trust, disclaimed all or a substantial part of the retirement plan benefits (with the disclaimed amounts being payable to her children, possibly over many years), downsized her home to one worth $543,000 or less and gifted the difference in value between her old home (worth $750,000) and her new home to her children (or contributed such difference to an appropriately drafted trust), she would have been eligible for free nursing home care. Following Eleanor's death, estate recovery would be possible with respect to assets retained, including the equity in her home. If Eleanor instead (on a timely basis) sold her home, transferred the proceeds to her children or an appropriately drafted trust and then leased a home, estate recovery could have been avoided. However, only clearly lawful planning activities should be undertaken. Legal guidance should be sought with respect to such matters.

Chapter 6

Charity and Legislative Proposals

Charity. Make no mistake about it, charity is great. A large percentage of the American population wants to assist those less fortunate than them. There is *absolutely nothing* wrong with charity. It is only good.

Contributions to most charities are tax deductible if the charity meets the specifications of Internal Revenue Code Section 501(c)(3). There are annual limits on deductions. Contributions to public charities generally are deductible up to 50 percent of AGI, while contributions to private foundations are often deductible to a lesser degree. (A public charity receives a certain minimum level of support from the general public, governments and charities. A private foundation does not receive such a minimum level of support.) Generally speaking, a tax-deductible contribution is available for the full cost of appreciated property, such as common stock of a publicly traded company. Gain on appreciated property is not required to be recognized for income tax purposes upon a gift to charity.

The impact of charity is a reduction in the difficulties of life for lower-income persons. Many charities supply food, shelter, utilities coverage and clothing to lower-income persons, thus increasing their standard of living. However, middle-class persons are beyond the scope of potential aid. Thus, they don't receive these benefits. The impact of them not receiving these benefits while lower-income persons receive them is a narrowing of the gap between lower-income persons and middle-income persons or, as noted above, an increasing of the lifestyle gap in favor of lower-income persons over middle-income persons falling within the lower end of the middle-income spectrum.

To the skeptical reader, this is all hogwash. It is math and finance. It's also true.

To the liberal-minded, the obvious answer is: Expand the entitlements so net cash flow always increases. The conservative might reply: Reduce the entitlements, or instead shift some entitlements from lower-income persons to middle-income persons so that lifestyle only increases (or at least never decreases) as income increases. Given the financial problems of the country, it would seem that the latter approach would be the more reasonable of the two options.

Legislative Proposals. There is now a push by many Democrats to provide greater equalization of pay among Americans. Some proposals include increase in the minimum wage. Another proposal involves expansion of the earned income tax credit. A somewhat radical tax reform proposal that has been around for approximately 15 years is the "Fair Tax," which would replace the income tax, payroll taxes (FICA and Medicare), and the estate and gift tax with a national retail sales tax. Each possibility is discussed below.

Given "the ditch," an increase in the minimum wage could actually result in a decreased lifestyle for some people who experience a wage increase, absent correlative entitlements reform. It could also decrease employment of low-skilled workers. For example, some restaurants are now using iPads to relay orders to the kitchen, thereby reducing the number of servers needed to operate. However, without entitlements reform, an increase in the minimum wage would generally result in more cash flow (and a higher standard of living) to persons paid the minimum wage. However, studies show that a large percentage of persons paid the minimum wage are students.

Increasing the earned income tax credit would increase cash flow to persons who work. Since the credit is not counted as income for purposes of most or perhaps all entitlements, increasing it would only result in more cash flow to eligible recipients.

The Fair Tax bill includes a 23 percent "tax-inclusive" rate, meaning the actual tax rate on a tax-exclusive basis (i.e., the manner in which sales taxes are usually expressed) would be 29.9 percent. However, according to a 1999 study by the nonpartisan Joint Committee on Taxation, the revenue-neutral tax-exclusive rate would be 59.5 percent for the first five years after enactment and 57 percent thereafter. A substantial "prebate" (or advanced rebate) exists to pay fixed entitlement amounts to all households, in attempt to prevent the poor from paying any tax.

The Fair Tax would be a much simpler system than the current tax system. It is designed (although not admittedly) to shift a substantial part of the tax burden now borne by the wealthy and the upper middle class to the middle class and retirees. For retirees who lived and worked a career while the income tax system was in effect but now pay little or no tax, double taxation would the end result of the Fair Tax. Middle-class persons would pay more tax than they currently pay, making the ditch a bit deeper.

Because a revenue-neutral Fair Tax would shift a very substantial part of the federal tax burden from a small portion of the voting population to a large portion of the voting population, the odds of enactment of the Fair Tax (or of it being seriously proposed) are nil. However, given that virtually every other industrialized nation has both an income tax and a sales tax or a value-added tax (VAT), there is a very good chance that a VAT will be enacted at some time in the future to supplement the income tax. Like a sales tax, a VAT is a regressive tax. Generally speaking, the addition of a VAT would reduce all persons' net cash flow (and living standard). However, a VAT could possibly be implemented in a manner so that some incurred a relatively smaller (or larger) burden than others.

If a VAT was enacted, it would likely start with a very small rate and numerous exemptions (as most taxes do). Over time, the rate would increase and exemptions would diminish as federal spending increased.

The 2005 report of the President's Advisory Panel on Federal Tax Reform stated regarding a VAT: "The VAT has been adopted by every major developed economy except the United States." Interestingly, many people in the United States think a VAT will never exist. Currently, there is no serious discussion of a VAT in Congress.

If a VAT was ultimately enacted, an important question would be what impact would it have on the income tax system? If the income tax system would basically remain as it has been (with most seniors paying little or no tax), then traditional planning does not change. However, planning becomes very difficult if the traditional income tax system was to change (or could potentially change). Given the political clout of seniors and their growing numbers, it is unlikely that any future tax system changes will hit them hard.

With gridlock, the need to satisfy special interest groups and fear of losing seniors' votes, it now appears unlikely either of the two major parties will do anything to reduce federal spending to any significant degree in the near term. However, with the Democrats tending to favor lower- and middle-income households as well as seniors (who would bear much of the burden of a VAT), and Republicans courting seniors as well and claiming to despise any tax, it appears a VAT (if one should ever exist) is a long ways off. In other countries, the political group adding a VAT has been swept from power. In the current economic climate, it is doubtful many members of Congress wish to seek work in the private sector. Instead, tremendously increased debt is the likely result in the near term.

User fees and excise taxes aside, there are four common tax types:

- Income tax

- Sales and use taxes (or a VAT)

- Property tax

- Transfer tax (estate and gift tax)

Since World War II, the United States government has drawn the vast majority of its revenue from income taxes (including Social Security taxes and Medicare taxes). If in the future it remains as it has been since the income tax was enacted in 1913 (i.e., there are income taxes but no federal sales taxes or VAT), and spending on entitlements won't be cut substantially, then, absent a collapse, it is highly likely that income tax rates will increase substantially at some point in the future. However, given the political clout of seniors and the vast number of baby boomers, one would wonder whether a "carve out" from rate increases would exist for seniors.

For comparative purposes, adjusted for inflation by the Consumer Price Index (CPI), the 1954 federal income tax rate on taxable income in excess of $66,866 was 34 percent. Adjusted for inflation, the 1954 income tax rate on taxable income in excess of $133,728 was 50 percent. Looking back, since 1954 but prior to 1981, adjusted for inflation, the rates system (which often changed) was typically much more like the 1954 Code's rates system than today's rates system. Regarding deductions, in some ways there were more in 1954 (e.g., greater deductibility of interest expense) and in some ways there were less (e.g., depreciation). Today, the highest incremental federal tax rate is 39.6 percent. However, an additional 3.8 percent tax can apply to certain investment income on high income taxpayers, bringing the current highest total federal rate to 43.4 percent. (An additional tax of 0.9 percent applies to wages and self-employment income in excess of a threshold amount —$200,000 for single persons; $250,000 for married persons.) Because the current highest incremental tax rate for corporations is relatively high by world standards (35 percent), it is unlikely that any increases in corporate tax rates will be made.

Chapter 7

The Primary Entitlements and Tax Credits

Below is a list of the primary entitlements and many significant tax credits that impact a large percent of the American population. There are many other entitlements and tax credits under the federal umbrella. The authors, who have a substantial amount of financial education between them, believe the system is a complex mess. In this regard, the *Congressional Research Service* noted the following in a January 31, 2011 publication by Karen Spar titled "Federal Benefits and Services for People with Low Income: Programs, Policy, and Spending, FY2008-FY2009":

- It is important to note that the definitions of countable income also vary. Some programs have explicit rules for counting income while many do not. . . . [R]eaders should know there may be differences between programs, so that income counted in determining eligibility for one program might not be counted in another, even though the programs might appear to use similar eligibility criteria.

- Benefits provided under means-tested programs often—but not always—are excluded from the definition of income when determining eligibility for another means-tested program.

- Moreover, income (and assets, as discussed below), used to determine *eligibility* for a particular program might be evaluated differently when determining *benefit levels* under that program. Individuals with the same amount of countable income or assets might qualify for different levels of benefits, because of the program's specific calculation rules.

Earned Income Tax Credit (or Earned Income Credit – "EITC") — The EITC is a refundable tax credit paid to persons whose income is relatively low. It is designed to increase cash to people who work. The credit is refundable, meaning it will be paid to the taxpayer if it exceeds tax liability. The credit decreases as income increases. It increases with family size. The IRS provides online guidance concerning the credit, including Publication 596. There are private company-produced online calculators that calculate the credit, although some of them may not be accurate. According to the

CBO, the EITC, child care and other similar credits cost the federal government approximately $84 billion in 2013.

Obamacare (ACA) credit — The formula for Obamacare premium tax credits is provided in Internal Revenue Code Section 36B. These credits are refundable. In substance, they reduce the health care premium costs to the individual or household. The credit is based on the second lowest price for silver coverage in the geographic area where the individual or family resides. Obamacare provides for platinum, gold, silver, and bronze coverage options, with the expected actuarial out-of-pocket costs increasing as the metal value decreases. Silver coverage must be chosen in order for the credit to be available. As income increases, the credit amount decreases. The credit begins at 100 percent when income equals the FPL. The credit fully phases out at 400 percent of the FPL. Income is modified adjusted gross income (MAGI). For most persons, MAGI is adjusted gross income (AGI). According to a Bloomberg Businessweek article by Caroline Chen dated February 20, 2014 and titled, "Obamacare Consumers Avoiding Cheapest Health Plans," a U.S. Department of Human Services report stated that 62 percent of Obamacare enrollees have chosen mid-level silver plans. Thus, the premium credits appear to be attracting consumers.

In 2012, the U.S. Supreme Court ruled in *National Federation of Independent Businesses, et al. v. Sebelius* that Obamacare was constitutional. Part of Obamacare provides for expansion of Medicaid eligibility to persons and families with income not exceeding 138 percent of the Federal Poverty Level (FPL) and effectively conditions receipt of federal Medicaid funds on expansion of eligibility. However, as part of the Supreme Court decision, the Court ruled that the states could decide whether to expand Medicaid coverage to persons and families with income not exceeding 138 percent of the FPL without losing federal funding for Medicaid. According to CMS, as of October 24, 2013, a slight majority of states had adopted Obamacare's expansion of Medicaid.

Under the individual mandate of Obamacare, certain individuals who lack a certain minimum amount of health care coverage are required to obtain a minimum level of coverage or be subject to penalties. It is the individual mandate that was primarily in issue in the *National Federation of Independent Businesses* case. The monthly penalty amount with respect to a taxpayer who fails to maintain minimum essential coverage is the one-twelfth of the greater of a flat dollar amount for each uninsured person required to be insured (generally, all family members) or a percentage of household income in excess of the tax filing threshold. However, the total flat dollar amount cannot exceed 300 percent of the flat dollar amount for one person, and the flat dollar amount for dependents under the age of 18 is one-half of the ordinary amount. Also, the penalty amount cannot exceed the average national annual premium for qualified health plans that offer bronze-level coverage for the family size through an Obamacare exchange. For 2014, the flat dollar amount is $95. For 2015, the flat dollar amount is $325. In 2016, it is $695. Thereafter, the $695 amount is adjusted for inflation. The percentage of household income is 1.0 percent for 2014, 2.0 percent for 2015 and 2.5 percent thereafter. The penalty cannot be collected via lien or levy. Prior to the *National Federation of Independent Businesses* decision, controversy existed over whether it was a tax. (The ruling held that it was a tax.) However, it is unclear how the IRS can collect it if the taxpayer has not overpaid his tax liability for one or more years.

Generally, under Obamacare, midsized and large-sized employers must provide minimum essential health coverage to their employees or potentially be subject to penalties of $166.67 per month per full-time employee for failure to do so. For this purpose, as of February of 2014, for any given year beginning in 2015 for large employers (100 or more full-time employee equivalents) and beginning in 2016 for midsized employers (50-99 full-time employee equivalents), an employer generally is subject to Obamacare's minimum coverage requirements if it employed at least 50 full-time employee equivalents on average in the preceding year. (Whether lawful or not, the Obama Administration has delayed the effective dates. Certain requirements must be met in order for a midsize employer to delay applicability of the rules until 2016.) To calculate the number of employee equivalents for purposes of the 50 full-time employees test, for each month, the number of full-time employees is added to a number produced by dividing the hours worked by individuals who are not full-time employees by 120. An individual is a full-time employee for any month that he is employed on average 30 hours per week. Affiliated employers (through stock or other equity ownership) are aggregated and treated as one employer for testing purposes.

As previously noted, employees who receive *affordable* minimum essential coverage from their employers are not eligible to purchase coverage on an exchange, and therefore are not eligible for the premium credits. The determination of what is affordable is complex. Generally, the employee's required contribution cannot exceed 9.5 percent of household income. If affordable minimum essential coverage is not provided, then penalties can potentially apply to the employer.

Housing (Section 8) — Generally speaking, to qualify, household income must be 50 percent or less of the median income in the applicable county or metropolitan area. Local public housing agencies (PHAs) run the program. Vouchers are provided to eligible persons. A PHA must provide 75 percent of newly available vouchers to persons whose income does not exceed 30 percent of the median income amount for the area. Once eligible, eligibility remains until income exceeds 80 percent of the median income level for the area. So, once a person or household is eligible, there's a lot of leeway to earn more without losing the benefit. PHAs can set parameters on who is preferred for various reasons based on needs. An explanation of this program is provided at www.portal.hud.gov.

Generally, an eligible family unit must spend 30 percent of its adjusted income on rent. HUD pays the balance, and it generally pays it directly to the landlord. The PHA determines whether a particular rental property meets HUD's standards. It also determines if rent is in line. If not, the property can still be rented, but the tenant must pay the excess of the rental amount over the amount the PHA deems reasonable. However, a family cannot pay more than 40 percent of adjusted monthly income on rent. Generally, adjusted income is annual income (i.e., wages, salary, and nonmonetary income) minus an allowance of $480 per dependent family member. However, other deductions can further reduce adjusted monthly income.

The program is popular, and people wait in line to get the vouchers. Respectively, the 30 percent, 50 percent, and 80 percent figures for Atlanta-Sandy Springs-Marietta for a four-person household were $19,900, $33,150, and $53,050 in 2013. Regarding the definition of "income," all cash benefits, including unemployment compensation and Social Security (regardless of taxability), are counted. Financial aid for college is excluded. Most noncash forms of assistance are not counted. An adjustment (deduction) is available for child care expenses incurred to permit a household unit member to work or go to school. (This figure can be significant.) According to the OMB, federal housing assistance was budgeted to cost approximately $50 billion in 2013.

Utilities — LIHEAP (low-income home energy assistance program) provides utilities cost relief to low-income persons. The states administer it. In Georgia, the current annual amount is between $310 and $350.

Households with income below 60 percent of the state's median income (based on family size) qualify. For 2013, the cutoffs for Georgia were $21,029, $27,500, $33,970, $40,441, $46,912, and $53,382 for families of one, two, three, four, five and six people, respectively. According to the OMB, federal funding of LIHEAP was expected to cost the federal government approximately $4 billion in 2013.

College — Federal financial aid for college was thoroughly summarized in Chapter 4. Education tax credits are discussed below.

TANF — TANF stands for Temporary Assistance for Needy Families. It is welfare. While welfare was prevalent prior to significant reforms in the 1990s, in recent years, the prevalence of traditional welfare has diminished substantially. However, the other entitlements discussed herein, including SNAP, have been greatly expanded in recent years. The Georgia Department of Human Services (DHS) website notes that there were 3,442 adults receiving TANF benefits in 2011, and the total case number was then 19,256. According to the OMB, TANF and similar support programs were budgeted to cost the federal government approximately $21 billion in 2013.

Medicaid — As previously noted, the U.S. Supreme Court decision of 2012 regarding the constitutionality of Obamacare permitted states to reject ACA's expansion requirement of Medicaid to 138 percent of the FPL. ACA originally required the expansion, and federal law generally provides that a state must do what the federal government says in order to receive the federal Medicaid funds. The Supreme Court ruled that a state's (continued) receipt of Medicaid funding could not be conditioned on its expansion. Those states that did not expand in the initial years will not receive federal funding that would have fully covered the expansion. The "Subsidy Calculator" of the Kaiser Family Foundation website (http://kff.org/interactive/subsidy-calculator/) was used to provide all of the Obamacare premiums and premium tax credit figures produced in this book. (The zip code used was 30126.)

Georgia has (as of February of 2014) rejected Obamacare's expansion of Medicaid. Many states have done the same. In Georgia, pregnant women and infants under age 1 qualify for Medicaid if family income is at or below 200 percent of the FPL. For this purpose, pregnant women count as two (or more) family members. Georgia children up to age 1 are entitled to coverage if family income does not exceed 185 percent of the FPL.

Georgia children from age 1 to age 5 qualify if their family income does not exceed 133 percent of the FPL. Georgia children ages 6 to 18 qualify for Medicaid if their family income does not exceed the FPL. Also, children ages 6 to 18 who are not eligible for Medicaid can qualify for low-cost Right from the Start Medicaid (RSM) if their family income does not exceed 185 percent of the FPL. People who qualify for RSM are basically entitled to all necessary health care. Georgia residents who are either citizens or lawful residents potentially qualify for these benefits. Eligibility is confirmed semiannually by DFCS.

Obamacare Cost Sharing Subsidies - Obamacare provides for cost sharing subsidies to reduce the costs of health care of individuals and families with income between 100 percent and 250 percent of the FPL. Like many entitlements, the subsidies decrease as income increases. The subsidies cover part of deductibles, co-insurance and co-pays, to reduce the out-of-pocket costs of health care. The subsidies are designed to reduce the actuarial cost of health care (i.e., the average amount anticipated to be spent, using actuarial principles) to each covered person or household. For household income equal to or greater than to 100 percent of the FPL but not in excess of 150 percent of the FPL, the actuarial coverage percent is 94.

For household income greater than 150 of the FPL but not in excess of 200 percent of the FPL, the actuarial coverage percent is 87. For household income greater than 200 percent of the FPL but not in excess of 250 percent of the FLP, the actuarial coverage percent is 73. Thus, for example, for a household with income equal to 125 percent of the FPL, the expected out-of-pocket costs for health care would be six percent of the total costs.

For Indians who are enrolled in any qualified health plan in the individual market through an Obamacare exchange, there must be no cost sharing whatsoever if household income does not exceed 300 percent of the FPL. This perk is one of a *tremendous* number of special entitlements available only to Indians. For this purpose, Indians are persons who are members of an Indian tribe that is recognized as eligible for special programs and services under the U.S. Code (Title 25, Section 450b).

The State Children's Health Insurance Program (SCHIP) was enacted by Congress in 1997 to provide greater funding for health care for lower-income persons. It has been expanded by Congress. Basically, states were given the option to increase the Medicaid income coverage level or provide a new, separate insurance program. Most states increased the income coverage level to two times the FPL. Georgia did not do so. Instead,

Georgia adopted Peachcare, which supplies low-cost health care coverage to children who live in families not eligible for Medicaid but whose household income does not exceed 235 percent of the FPL. According to the CBO, SCHIP payments for 2013 totaled approximately $9 billion.

Georgia also provides cash assistance to lower-income working persons to help with the costs of child care. The payments by the Childcare and Parent Services Program (CAPS) have averaged $268 per month in recent years.

Head Start — The Head Start program essentially offers preschool and related nutrition and dental services. It is available to children in families whose income level does not exceed the FPL. Families whose income does not exceed 130 percent of the FPL can also qualify.

Voluntary Medicare Prescription Drug Benefit — This entitlement is available to seniors and people with disabilities. Non-disabled seniors with incomes no higher than 150 percent of the FPL potentially qualify. Persons eligible for Medicaid or SSI automatically qualify. Those persons with income no greater than 135 percent of the FPL receive the greatest level of subsidies. In 2009, 10 million people received subsidies.

Lifeline cell phone — Lifeline entitles the beneficiary to a free cell phone and 250 minutes of cell phone use each month. Additional minutes can be purchased for very little cost. To participate, income must not exceed 135 percent of FPL or the person must be eligible for any one of the following programs: Medicaid, SNAP, SSI, Section 8 housing, LIHEAP, TANF, free school lunches, Head Start, or one or more of a few other programs. Income is taxable income, and the FPL is based on family size. Income includes ordinary cash inflow, including unemployment compensation. Public assistance benefits are also included. Specifically excluded from income are federal financial aid and income from occasional jobs.

One phone is allowed per family. Ninety-two percent of lower-income households receive the benefit. The funding source is the Federal Universal Service Fund, which is funded by fees charged to people who use phones and pay for service plans. Often, the fees are listed as a separate line item on a phone bill.

Food — Like health care, a variety of programs provide food. Under the Child and Adult Care Food Program (CACFP), children under age 12 and elderly adults are eligible for free meals and snacks if their income is below 135 percent of the FPL. Reduced-cost meals and snacks are available if income does not exceed 185 percent of the FPL. Families who receive SNAP or TANF are automatically eligible. Head Start-eligible children are also eligible.

The Supplemental Nutrition Assistance Program (SNAP) provides food stamps. Households must not have countable assets in excess of $2,000 if under age 60, or $3,250 if over age 59. Home value is excluded. Retirement plan and IRA assets are also excluded. In 39 states, the value of all vehicles is excluded. In 11 states, the value of one vehicle is excluded. Gross and net income tests apply for SNAP benefits. However, elderly persons and disabled persons need only meet a net income test.

Generally, non-disabled persons between age 16 and 60 must either work, accept suitable employment, or participate in training programs for work to be eligible. While retirement plan assets are excluded from the assets calculations, the income from such a plan (or from an IRA) would be counted for purposes of the income test. Income that is counted includes all traditional taxable income, including pensions and unemployment compensation. Excluded from income are noncash income, housing subsidies, education assistance, and certain "irregular income."

Under the gross income test, gross income of the family unit cannot exceed 130 percent of the FPL. Under the net income test, net income cannot exceed the FPL. Figures are calculated monthly. The following monthly deductions are permitted for 2014: 20 percent of earned income, a standard deduction of $152 for a family size of one to three people and $163 for a family of four, dependent care expenses when needed for work or for going to school, child support payments, and an "excess shelter" deduction. (Higher standard deductions are available for families with more than four persons, and for people living in Alaska or Hawaii.) The excess shelter deduction is available if more than half of a household's income is used to pay utilities, phone, and rent or mortgage payments. Generally, the deduction (which is the excess amount) is limited to $478. The monthly net income is multiplied by 0.3 to produce the amount the family must pay for SNAP benefits. There are fixed "allotments" of benefits, from which the family's required contribution is deducted to produce the monthly benefit. The maximum monthly allotments are $189, $347, $497, $632, $750, $900, and $1,137 for families of one to seven members. An additional $142 of allotment per member is permitted for families with more than seven members.

As long as the eligibility requirements continue to be met, SNAP benefits can be received indefinitely. The number of persons participating has exploded nationally from approximately 32 million in 2008 to approximately 47 million in 2013. Thus, while traditional welfare has significantly decreased, other entitlements like SNAP have taken traditional welfare's place. According to the CBO, $83 billion of SNAP benefits were provided in 2013.

WIC — The Special Supplemental Nutrition Program for Women, Infants, and Children (WIC) provides benefits to low-income women, infants, and children. Women generally qualify while pregnant and up to six weeks after giving birth. Infants qualify up until their first birthday. Children qualify up until age 5. Basically, WIC provides free healthy food to people who are potentially subject to nutrition risk. A physician or nurse must determine whether the person is eligible. Income limits are set at the state level. However, people receiving Medicaid, SNAP, or TANF automatically qualify.

The Commodity Supplemental Food Program (CSFP) — The CSFP provides free food to pregnant and breastfeeding women, infants, children up to age 6, and persons age 60 or older. The USDA purchases food and provides it to state agencies for distribution at centers. Generally, family income for elderly persons must be at or below 130 percent of the FPL. For women, infants, and children, the income level generally is 185 percent of the FPL. Women, infants, and children who receive Medicaid, SNAP, or TANF benefits are automatically eligible. According to the budgeted OMB, WIC and CSFP (combined) cost the federal government approximately $7 Billion in 2013.

School breakfast program — Children from families with household income at or below 130 percent of the FPL are eligible for free breakfasts at school. For children whose family income is between 130 and 185 percent of the FPL, the student is entitled to low-cost breakfasts. For these meals, the charge for a low-cost breakfast cannot be more than 30 cents. Through June 30, 2014, 130 percent of the PFL is $30,615 for a family of four (and the 185 percent amount is $43,568). The USDA provides the cash for the program. In the 2010 fiscal year, over 10.1 million children received a free or reduced-cost lunch. It has been reported by more than one source that the program is not audited.

School lunch program — The eligibility standards are the same as those for the school breakfast program. The lunch cost for those children whose families fall in the 130–185 percent range cannot exceed 40 cents. Schools are also entitled (by law) to "entitlement" foods at a value of 23.25 cents per meal. They can also qualify for "bonus" USDA foods when they are available from surplus agricultural stocks. According to the CBO, child nutrition programs cost the federal government approximately $20 billion in 2013.

Nursing Home care — Similar to college financial aid, nursing home care is discussed in Chapter 4.

Child Tax Credits — The child tax credit is claimed by filing Form 8812 with one's Form 1040. Somewhat unsurprisingly, calculation of the credit is complex. The ordinary credit is $1,000 per child, and it is partially refundable. The child must not have attained the age of 17 before the end of the tax year in order to be considered for the credit. Eligibility for the credit phases out as income increases. For single taxpayers for 2013, the phase-out begins at $75,000 of modified AGI. For taxpayers married filing jointly for 2013, the phase-out begins at $110,000. The phase-out amounts to a $50 reduction for each $1,000 or fraction thereof of modified AGI in excess of the threshold. For most persons, modified AGI is AGI. The credit is refundable in an amount equal to the lesser of the unclaimed portion of the nonrefundable credit amount or 15 percent of the taxpayer's earned income in excess of $3,000. Taxpayers with three of more children may use an alternative means of calculating the refundable child credit. The refundable portion of the credit is sometimes called the "additional child tax credit."

American Opportunity Tax Credit — This credit reduces tax liability and, to a certain degree, cash payments if the credit exceeds tax liability for college costs for each student. The credit is 100 percent of the first $2,000 of college expenses for each student, plus 25 percent of the next $2,000 of expenses. Up to 40 percent of the credit is refundable, meaning it will be paid to the taxpayer(s) if tax liability is exceeded. The credit phases out as income increases. The credit phases out between $80,000 and $90,000 of modified adjusted gross income (typically equal to AGI) for single filers and $160,000 to $180,000 of MAGI for joint filers. However, the education expenses potentially subject to the credit are reduced by tax-free educational assistance received, including Pell grants. For purposes of both this credit and the Lifetime Learning Credit, amounts sourced from Section 529 plans are not eligible expenses.

Lifetime Learning Credit — This credit is available on an individual basis. The maximum credit for any year is $2,000. It does not vary by family size. The credit is 20 percent of the first $10,000 spent on qualified education at a qualified educational institution. Eligibility for the credit phases out as income increases. For 2014, the phase-out occurs between $54,000 and $64,000 of MAGI for single filers and $108,000 to $128,000 of MAGI for married filing jointly taxpayers. The credit is coordinated with the American Opportunity Tax Credit, such that a taxpayer can elect to receive one or the other (but not both) in any given tax year.

Retirement Savings Contributions (Saver's) Tax Credit — The saver's tax credit is available for contributions to 401(k) plans, similar elective deferral plans and IRAs for certain persons. The annual credit is a percent of the amount contributed to an IRA or 401(k) plan, up to $2,000. The percent decreases as AGI increases. For 2014, for married persons filing jointly, the credit is 50 percent if AGI does not exceed $36,000, 20 percent for AGI between 36,000 and $39,000, and 10 percent for AGI above $39,000 but not in excess of $60,000. For single persons, the credit is 50 percent if AGI does not exceed $18,000, 20 percent if AGI is between $18,000 and $19,500, and 10 percent if AGI is greater than $19,500 but not more than $30,000.

Child and Dependent Care Credit — A tax credit is available for costs paid for childcare for children under age 13, if the childcare is necessary for the taxpayer (or spouse, if married and a joint return is filed) to be able to work or look for work. The maximum amount that is considered for the credit is $3,000 for one child and $6,000 for two or more children. The credit is nonrefundable. The credit percentage decreases as AGI increases. If AGI does not exceed $15,000, the credit percentage is 35. For taxpayers with AGI in excess of $15,000, the credit percent is decreased by one percentage point for each $2,000 or fraction thereof of AGI in excess of $15,000. However, the minimum credit percent is 20, and it applies to taxpayers with AGI in excess of $43,000 in 2013.

Social Security — Social Security is the largest entitlement program of the federal government. It is an involuntary pension system. Social Security is also a "pay as you go system," whereby current beneficiaries receive their benefits from Social Security taxes paid by current workers. Substantially all the benefits are currently funded by payroll taxes. The tax rate is 6.2 percent of wages, and it applies to both employer and employee, up to the Social Security Wage Base in any given year. For 2014, the Social Security Wage Base is $117,000. For self-employed persons in 2014, the tax rate is 12.4 percent, and it applies to self-employment income up to $117,000. According to the Summary of the 2013 Annual Social Security and Medicare Trust Fund Reports, for 2012, the Old-Age and Survivors Insurance (OASI) and Social Security Disability Income (DI) costs were, respectively, $637.9 billion and $136.9. For 2013, the CBO reported these amounts as, respectively, $668 billion and $140 billion.

For decades beginning in the 1980s, Social Security ran surpluses. The surpluses were loaned to the General Fund. Thus, there is a theoretical surplus of over $2 trillion in the Social Security trust fund. However, there are no assets that secure this fund. Rather, the fund merely possesses IOUs from the General Fund. In the future, the IOUs will need to be repaid from taxes or more debt. Recently, the system has been in the process of reversing, such that annual outlays exceed annual inflows. Due to the growing number of baby boomer retirements, future revenue is not expected to ever exceed future expenditures. And the ratio of workers to retirees is expected to slowly decline. By approximately 2040, revenue is expected to equal approximately 75 percent of expenditures, with little change thereafter.

From a benefits perspective, Social Security is very progressive. The current formula is provided at www.socialsecurity.gov. Basically, each person grows his or her annual earnings by an inflation factor and then uses the 35 years with the highest amount of "indexed earnings" to compute the benefit. The "high 35" years of indexed earnings is divided by 420 to produce average monthly indexed earnings. This figure is then subjected to the following formula to produce the normal retirement age benefit: (a) the first $816 is multiplied by .9; (b) the next $4,101 is multiplied by .32; and (c) the amount in excess of $4,917 is multiplied by .15. The benefit is reduced for early retirement. For example, a person born in 1952 would have a normal retirement age of 66, and would experience a 25 percent reduction if benefits commenced at the earliest retirement age (62). Cost of living adjustments (COLAs) are ordinarily given to Social Security beneficiaries. However, in recent years, COLAs have not always been given. COLAs are tied to inflation.

Social Security also provides disability benefits. While these benefits are beyond the scope of this text, abuses of the disability program in recent years have been well documented.

Medicare — Medicare is a partially voluntary, partially involuntary health care system for retirees. A dedicated tax exists equal to 1.45 percent of compensation on employer and employee (2.9 percent of self-employment income for self-employed persons) to fund Part A of Medicare (hospitals, hospice, home health, etc.). Unlike Social Security, there is no cap on compensation (or self-employment income) subject to the tax. Practically, most of the remainder of Medicare is funded through the General Fund (and through general tax revenues). Due to the retirement of the baby boomers and the constantly increasing cost of health care (at a rate greater than the ordinary inflation rate), it is growing at a much greater rate than Social Security.

Part B of Medicare mainly covers doctor visits, supplies, procedures, and tests. Technically, there is a Part B trust fund. Practically, the benefits are supplied by premiums paid by beneficiaries and the General Fund. Beneficiaries generally also pay a small portion of the Medicare-approved cost for services, procedures, and the like.

Part C of Medicare is coverage through HMOs and private insurance preferred provider organizations (PPOs). It is similar to coverage supplied by many employers. Basically, the federal government and the beneficiary pay the cost of coverage.

Part D of Medicare relates to prescription drugs. It is partially paid for by individuals who participate. Part D was added by Republicans in 2003, when they controlled the Congress and the White House. Obamacare significantly expanded Part D coverage.

Other costly entitlements include pensions for government workers and military personnel. According to the CBO, these costs for 2013 were, respectively, $92 billion and $54 billion. Income security benefits for veterans totaled $66 billion in 2013. SSI benefits for 2013 cost $53 billion. Approximately $69 billion of unemployment compensation was paid in 2013.

Appendix

Numerous assumptions were made in producing the figures found in charts and graphs supplied in this book. These assumptions are provided below.

For taxes, it was assumed that the only income was earned income from employment (or self-employment) and, except as noted otherwise, the only deductions were the standard deduction and personal exemptions. While some persons with income above the ditch level would have had deductions that would have reduced their liabilities, many or perhaps most of the people in the ditch (or with less income) would not have had such deductions. The 2013 Drake software system was used to produce the tax figures. Most figures were verified by a computer application created by one of the co-authors. "FICA" includes both Social Security tax (at a rate of 6.2 percent) and Medicare health insurance (HI) tax (at a rate of 1.45 percent).

As previously noted, the Obamacare premiums and credits were produced by utilizing the website of The Kaiser Family Foundation. The website is http://kff.org/interactive/subsidy-calculator/. The zip code used was 30126 (a zip code for Cobb County, Georgia).

Section 8 housing was calculated assuming a home with a PHA-approved rental amount of $1,100 per month. In the charts and graphs, home rental cost is assumed to be $1,100 per month. The metropolitan area utilized was Atlanta-Sandy Springs-Marietta, Georgia. The deductions taken to produce the amount of rent required by the tenant under Section 8 were the minimum possible. For example, in the family of four chart, $480 of deductions were taken for each of the three dependents (for a total of $1,440).

The school food figures were taken directly from the U.S. Department of Agriculture's website regarding the entitlement and the Cobb County website regarding meal prices for the 2013–14 school year. For children not eligible for the entitlements, the same cost figures were used.

SNAP (food stamps) benefits were calculated as follows: All income received was assumed to be compensation. For a family of four, assumed child care costs were $200 per month. For a family of three, assumed child care costs were $300 per month. No other deductions (other than automatic deductions) were taken. Thus, the SNAP benefits provided in charts found in this book likely are less than what would be available. Also, no CACFP benefits were deemed to exist. The SNAP assets requirements were assumed to be met by those persons receiving benefits.

The cell phone cost of $35 per month is a rough average of the cost that would be charged by a cell phone company to provide 250 cell phone minutes, including taxes and fees, plus the costs of renting or purchasing a basic cell phone. This figure is an estimate as, outside of Lifeline, few companies offer a plan that provides exactly 250 minutes of cell phone use.

The food figures are based on the U.S. Bureau of Labor Statistics average annual costs of food (in the home and eat out) for an average household for 2012. The total cost was $6,599. The average household size in the U.S. varies by income amount, but a rough average of three is approximately correct, and it was used to produce the figures. Thus, for a family of four, the figure used ($8,799) is $6,599 multiplied by 1.3333.

Utilities are a rough average based on the cost of utilities for a three-bedroom, two-bathroom home located in zip code 30126. The utilities include gas, electric, and water/sewer. The LIHEAP figure of $330 is the approximate average annual amount of benefits provided in Georgia.

Regarding the lengthy cash balance plan example in the Planning section of Chapter 5, the following analysis was applied: Regarding federal financial aid for college, because the cash balance plan is not an elective deferral plan (i.e., it has a fixed allocation formula, as it must under the tax-qualified plan rules), it is very likely that the amounts contributed each year would be excluded from the income calculations. The exclusion (compared to the result if nothing had been done) results in a net income reduction of $52,617 each year when taxes are considered. Furthermore, the pension benefits would be excluded from the net worth analysis, whereas any investments that would have been purchased (e.g., assuming here, in a Section 529 plan), in lieu of the cash balance plan investments would have been counted in net worth calculations. Assuming the annual investments would have been $42,267 per year (based on a netting of the $66,000 and tax benefits related thereto), and assuming 6 percent compounding, the amount accumulated over four years would have been approximately $184,902. To produce the average over four years, this figure is divided by two, resulting in $92,451. To this figure was added the average value of the existing assets of $100,000, assuming a 25 percent effective tax rate applied to the $25,000 of ordinary investments and no taxes applied to the $75,000 of Section 529 plan assets. Again, 6 percent annual compounding was applied. Using this net worth change figure and the reduced income figure described above ($52,730) produced an annual EFC decrease due to using the cash balance plan (in lieu of doing nothing) of $25,151. Here, total college costs equaled $50,000. Adding the tax savings, the total annual savings is $48,884. Applying these total savings for four years, the total saved would be $195,536 (i.e., $48,884 x 4). The itemized deduction figure for the cash balance approach was assumed to be $25,000. The "do nothing" approach has a $3,393 greater state tax amount due to the increased taxable income (thus resulting in the assumed figure of $28,393).

The graphs and charts do not take into account Obamacare cost sharing subsidies. As noted, these subsidies further reduce the costs of health care to individuals and families with income between 100 percent and 250 percent of the FPL. Also, it was assumed that the individuals would not be eligible to take a child and dependent care tax credit.

The analyses do not consider charitable contributions for the benefit of lower income persons.